Computing
in
Organizations

James B. Rule
Debra Gimlin
Sylvia J. Sievers

Computing
in
Organizations

Myth and Experience

Transaction Publishers
New Brunswick (U.S.A.) and London (U.K.)

Library of Congress Catalog Number: 2001057457
ISBN: 0-7658-0141-8
Printed in Canada

Library of Congress Cataloging-in-Publication Data

Rule, James B., 1943-
  Computing in organizations : myth and experience / James B. Rule,
  Debra Gimlin, Sylvia J. Sievers.
        p. cm.
  Includes bibliographical references and index.
  ISBN: 0-7658-0141-8 (cloth : alk. paper)
    1. Business—Data processing. 2. Management—Data processing.
  3. Communication in organizations—Data processing. I. Gimlin,
  Debra L., 1967- II. Sievers, Sylvia J. III. Title.

HF5548.2 .R76 2002
658'.05—dc21   2001057457

Contents

Acknowledgments

Many generous and thoughtful institutions and people have supported the work reported here over the nearly twenty years since it was first conceived. Among institutions, the National Science Foundation (in several separate grants) and the Russell Sage Foundation have provided crucial resources for the study. As for personal contributions, special recognition goes to Paul Attewell, who helped conceive the study in the early 1980s and set many of its crucial directions. In addition, many current and former colleagues at Stony Brook in the intervening years have provided advice and support. These include Stanley Feldman, Mark Granovetter, Nilufer Isvan, Jeanne Kidd, Timothy Moran, Frank Romo, Ian Roxborough, Warren Sanderson, Michael Schwartz, Andrea Tyree, and others. From outside Stony Brook, we have benefited from advice from Rob Kling, Robert K. Merton, Marcia Meyers, Patricia Roos, and others. We extend our sincere thanks to all these worthy individuals and institutions, none of whom can be considered responsible for any shortcomings in this work.

1

Introduction

What image, in the iconography of our times, is more evocative of social change than that of the computer? What technologies besides those of information do we more readily identify as transforming our social world from what it has been to what it will be? Whatever else we "know" about computing, we are convinced that it represents a sweeping force for social and economic change.

Whether such change is for the better or for the worse is a matter of vast and fruitful disagreement. But what passes unquestioned in these controversies is the assumption that the antagonists actually share—the belief in the social potency of information technologies. From learned specialists to ordinary citizens, the conviction is firm that the apparently never-ending growth in computing is bound to reshape both our most basic social and economic arrangements *and* our most fundamental thoughtways.

The force of these convictions in public affairs should not be missed. Consider the assumptions conveyed in these press accounts:

> The decline of California's education system...has appalled Susan Hammer, 55, who took office as San Jose's mayor three years ago. She thinks that computers in classrooms can help turn things around.
>
> San Jose has committed $1 million for the effort, which also has funding and support from many Silicon Valley companies....
>
> "Is it practical [asked interviewer Martha Groves] to have this kind of program when many people in America cannot read a bus schedule or even a "See Dick run" book? Is it really going to work?
>
> "From the little I know [replied Mayor Hammer], one of the ways to create a level playing field...in a classroom is to have all students have the same educational opportunities, and I think computers can provide that, where [students] have the opportunity to access the same kind of information, communicate between schools, access libraries around the country...."
>
> "Aren't people asking [the interviewer continued] whether the city can really afford to spend money on technology rather than school lunch programs, textbooks and athletics?

"I don't hear that [replied the Mayor]. Feedback has been positive...."—*Los Angeles Times*, 11 May 1994, p. D6

About 36% of Americans think that personal computers could solve the country's problems better than 100 politicians.

Techtel Corp., a marketing research firm in Emeryville, California, reported that statistic last week, based on a technology-use survey conducted in July, Knight-Ridder reports...

"Americans want good, quick decisions," said William LaWarre, president of Northlich Stolley LaWarre, a Cincinnati communications company that did the survey with Techtel. "These findings not only show how frustrated people are with political posturing, but they also demonstrate a new level of familiarity people have with personal computers."—*The Washington Post*, 29 January 1996, p. B17.

Everyone attentive to the mass media has heard at least a few stories like these—stories that attest to the extraordinary powers ascribed to computers in the reordering of human affairs. Many of these expectations, it should be noted, have to do with the role of computing in *organizations*—companies, government bureaucracies, not-for-profit agencies and the like. What we expect of organizations—from the IRS to credit card companies to the local drug store—clearly has everything to do with our belief that computers confer on such organizations unique and sweeping powers. Perhaps needless to say, the aims and ambitions of those who work in such organizations are shaped in turn by their expectations of what computing can do for them.

This book aims to help make sense of such expectations—by juxtaposing them with a systematic look at the realities of computing use in more than one hundred typical private-sector organizations. We have studied the role of computing in these establishments for over ten years, from the mid-1980s to the mid-1990s. This was a pivotal moment in the social history of the technology, a period when computing was evolving from a novelty to standard presence in most organizations.

Detailed interviews in these rank-and-file establishments have provided a picture of the actual roles played and purposes served by computers. How is computing actually being used? How has it changed the ways in which the people involved conceive what they do? How do the towering expectations of the powers of computing shape the efforts to mobilize the technology? What relationship is there between such expectations and the empirical record of practice in these organizations?

Even the mostly rank-and-file, unremarkable organizations making up our sample have repeatedly forced us to confront what we call the *mythology* of computing. We hardly doubt that computing embodies all sorts of objective powers—the power to organize work, or to revamp communication patterns, or to guide machines or to shape the management of databases. But we were not fully prepared for the sweeping and often uncritical certainties about the powers of computing that our interviewees conveyed to us. These expectations, we are convinced, represent a potent force in their own right for social change. Accordingly, we direct much attention in the pages that follow to what can precisely be called the mythology of computing.

Calling something a myth hardly amounts to labeling it as misleading, illusory or unworthy of belief. We invoke the term in its more precise sociological sense. By *myths*, we mean *ideas providing a common reference for interpreting experience or justifying conduct—yet entertained in such a way as to remain beyond the reach of critical correction.*

Far from being solely a source of error or a prop to superstition, myths in this sense are indispensable to social life. As de Tocqueville wrote, in a famous passage,

> If man were forced to demonstrate for himself all the truths of which he makes daily use, his task would never end... He is reduced to take on trust a host of facts and opinions which he has not had either the time or the power to verify for himself, but which men of greater ability have found out, or which the crowd adopts. ([1840] 1954, p. 9)

Tocqueville did not apply the term *myth* to beliefs "taken on trust" in this way, but the term fits.

De Tocqueville's insight has lost none of its importance with the passage of time. As we begin the twenty-first century, certainties about the forceful and transformative role of computing in human affairs play exactly the role he describes. Especially for a phenomenon as rich and complex as computing, there is often little choice but to rely on "a host of facts or opinions" about the technology that represents the standard wisdom of our culture. Fortunately, we have ample means to study such reliance, and the situations to which it is applied.

The Intellectual Pedigree

Where does today's mythology of computing power come from? Part of its origin undoubtedly lies in the scholarly vision of science

and technology projected in the eighteenth and nineteenth centu-
ries. The very founders of social science were convinced that scientific inquiry, and the tools and practices emerging from it, played
the most far-reaching role in reshaping social affairs.

For the earliest figures, these views were ultimately optimistic.
Saint-Simon and Comte identified scientific thinking as the key force
behind the movement from social systems based on custom, superstition, and inherited privilege to the rational social orders that they
saw being born. They foresaw a world where social arrangements
would be based on the same sorts of thinking underlying solutions
to scientific problems. The rise of science and technology, then,
would help engender a world in which human institutions, from the
workplace to the state, would more efficiently serve human interests. The profound optimism underlying this vision of the social
role of science and technology continues to animate much thinking
today.

For Marx—reacting in part to Saint Simon—matters were neither
quite so simple nor so encouraging. Like his predecessors, Marx
saw science and technology as propelling history forward—by fueling the rise of capitalism as the dominant force in the economy
and, ultimately, in all of social life. Modern industrial capitalism
without the scientific thinking and technological innovation inspired by it would simply have been unthinkable to Marx. To the
extent that capitalism flourished by rational planning and critical
judgment, its scientific spirit represented a positive force. But
the more immediate effects of science and technology on most
people were far more problematic. The innovative forces that
they unleashed afforded vast gains in productivity, and vast new
wealth—for a few. But ordinary workers would find themselves
robbed both of traditional skills and purchasing power by the onslaught of technology. Only when capitalism ultimately collapsed,
from its inability to govern the productive forces that it had unleashed, would the benefits of science and technology be available
to meet human needs.

Adam Smith, founder of another key social science tradition,
shared some of Marx's ambivalence, if not his prophecies. Smith,
too, acknowledged the far-reaching effects of science and technology in such realms as the rationalization of production through as-
sembly-line techniques. But he had no illusions that the immediate
effects of these innovations on ordinary producers would be be-

neficent. The assembly line, he noted, dulled the sensibilities of those who worked on it, even as it raised their productivity. Unlike Marx, Smith entertained no utopian expectation of a revolutionary reversal that would obviate the tradeoff between the objective efficiency of technology and its human costs.

* * *

These are classic voices of modern social science. Obviously, none of these authors knew anything about computing *per se*. Nevertheless, one cannot fail to be struck by the parallels between present-day writing on science and technology in general, and computing in particular, and these classic themes. In the array of commentary by present-day analysts, it is rare to find a line of argument not prefigured in pre-twentieth century writings on science and technology.

Daniel Bell's celebrated theories of post-industrial society, to take a notable example, have been aptly characterized as his "debate with the ghost of Saint Simon". The continuities in the two authors' writing are impossible to miss—for example, in Bell's vision of the role of *theoretical* thinking in shaping "post-industrial society":

> What is distinctive about the post-industrial society is the change in the character of knowledge itself. What has become decisive for the organization of decisions and the direction of change is the centrality of *theoretical* knowledge—the primacy of theory over empiricism and the codification of knowledge into abstract systems of symbols that...can be used to illuminate many different and varied areas of experience. (1973, p. 20)

A few pages later, Bell adds another idea with a Saint-Simonian pedigree—the notion that *new forms of thinking* are required for management of post-industrial social arrangements.

> The major social revolution of the latter half of the twentieth century is the attempt to master "scale" by new technological devices, whether it be "real-time" computer information or new kinds of quantitative programming. (p. 42)

By "scale" Bell means the sheer size and complexity of social organization.

If Bell upholds and extends the relatively optimistic perspectives of Saint Simon and Comte, Henry Braverman provides a late twentieth century voice for those of Marx. His remarks on computing in the following passage are simply concomitant of his view of the role of science and technology in the workplace more generally:

[A]s in manufacturing, the office computer does not become, in the capitalist mode of production, the giant step that it could be toward the dismantling and scaling down of the technical division of labor. Instead, capitalism goes against the grain of the technological trend and stubbornly reproduces the outmoded division of labor in a new and more pernicious form. (1974, pp. 223-230)

One could equally well cite other contemporary commentaries on computing which strike themes typical of Adam Smith, Herbert Spencer, Max Weber, or other classic figures in social thought.

The differences in these visions of the social roles of science and technology are profound. But note that all these traditional visions share two noteworthy assumptions. *First*, that the importance of science-based technologies in human affairs stems from their objective ability to provide superior solutions to demonstrable "problems" or needs. *Second*, that the application of these objective powers generates crucial "second order consequences" by reshaping the mind-sets of those employing them. Thus, the recourse to computing (or any other science-based technology) requires users to understand the world in different, presumably more rational, ways. This theme reasserts itself very broadly, all the way from the critical perspectives of Marx to the optimistic ones of Bell.

For most readers, such assumptions may appear as little more than common sense. But they hardly represent the only plausible organizing vision. Consider the view articulated by the French sociologist Jacques Ellul.

For Ellul and his followers, it might be said that invention is the mother of necessity. The technological mentality is not the result of the recourse to technology, so much as its cause. The availability of new technological possibilities does not so much fulfill existing needs as it creates such needs. Indeed, in this view, every technological innovation generates new needs, which in turn can only be satisfied with yet further technological innovation. Ellul might well have characterized the mentality driving technological innovation as a form of mythology. In fact, the term he chose was *technique*:

[T]echnique...poses primarily technical problems which consequently can be resolved only by technique. The present level of technique brings new advances, and these in turn add to existing technical difficulties and technical problems, which demand further advances still.... For example, to make housework easier, garbage-disposal units have been put into use which allow the garbage to run off through the kitchen sinks. The result is enormous pollution of the rivers. It is then necessary to find some new means of purifying the rivers so that water can be used for drinking. A great quantity of oxygen is required for bacteria to destroy these organic materials. And how shall we oxygenate rivers? This is an example of the way in which technique engenders itself." (1964, p. 92)

This is a jarring view of technological change. Instead of technology-as-a-source-of-solutions-to-human-problems, we have technology-as-an-equivalent-of-drug-addiction. For Ellul, the "needs" served by technology are themselves products of the same mind-set that insists on innovation. The more technological change is accepted as a source of "solutions" to human "problems," the more aspects of life are defined as "problematic."

Many readers will no doubt find this model absurd, if only because it flies in the face of many things that everyone "knows" about in regard to technological progress. We know—or we think that we know—that appendectomies offer an objectively superior solution to the problem of appendicitis; or that hybrid or genetically-engineered crops provide solutions to chronic food shortages; or that word-processing is demonstrably superior as a means of writing and editing than pen and paper, typewriters, and print. To suggest that the tools that we employ to satisfy these needs have somehow brought the needs into existence strains our credulity.

But perhaps it deserves to be strained. For many technologies, attention to the fine detail of their evolution and adoption suggests that Ellul's model may not be so absurd. In the case of computing, there is reason to believe that prevailing mythology should not always be "taken on trust," to use de Tocqueville's words. It would be rash, we think, to imagine that all the "needs" served by computing could have been documented before its rise.

Present-day Sources of Computing Mythology

Scholarly tradition, then, has helped inspire much present-day mythology on computing. But these ideas also have their origins in strictly contemporary sources. Magazines, movies, television and other mass media furnish a constant stream of dazzling images of the computerized future. Most readers have thus by now probably grown inured to prophecies like the following:

The technology that everyone's fantasizing about is virtual reality. The expectations for virtual reality are of Star Trek magnitude. Enter a room... Tell a computer to run the "OK Corral" program, and you're deposited the dusty Old West; with boots, bandanna, and six-gun, ready to take on Wyatt Earpp. It's all done with computer simulation, and it's as real as any reality.

> Today's virtual reality has not yet reached those expectations.... But virtual reality
> will grow up. The virtual site inspection will occur in our lifetime. Explore a facility
> without leaving your office. You like the ballroom, but need a stage at one end? Input
> the change. The stage appears. The computer sends the specs to a contractor. The stage
> is built before you arrive.
>   Virtual reality does have a downside. It could become society's next drug—the
> addict enjoying its pleasures to the point of never turning the computer off. (Ross
> Weiland in Kling, ed., 1995, p.65)

Accounts like these have conspired with more scholarly visions to foster a diffuse public credulity regarding computing. Writers, editors, producers, and other participants in public communication have grasped the fact that no social repercussions of information technology are too extreme to be entertained. For the publics subject to this onslaught, the cumulative effect is a certain suspension of disbelief. With computing, one comes to acknowledge that anything is possible.

Note that this mandate of credibility is not a general feature of beliefs about technology. We do not attribute such sweeping powers of social transformation to the technologies of mass transit, for example—or agricultural pest control, or weather prediction. Instead, we make the plausible assumption that the unfolding of the technologies in question may turn out more or less felicitously, with more or less far-reaching repercussions on human values and social arrangements. Perhaps just as importantly, we do not usually ascribe to these technologies the diffuse *fascination* that surrounds computing.

Our willingness to attribute transformative, engaging possibilities to computing, by contrast, seems all but endless. Indeed, public perceptions of computing have come to be governed by what we would call the Loch Ness Monster phenomenon. By this we mean the status of a topic as a virtually endless fount of gratifying speculation, regardless of the empirical basis for it. Thus, there appears only the slenderest reason to believe in the existence of the beast in Loch Ness, and much to doubt it. Yet discussion of the monster's possible form and habits will not die. The idea that there *could* be such a creature—never really disprovable—is simply too infinitely intriguing to be left alone. By contrast, the notion that no such beast exists, though probably true, is hopelessly lacking in charm. Books, articles, television documentaries, and the like on the *non-existence* of the monster—should any be presented—might have everything in their favor in terms of the weight of the evidence. But such conclusions will inevitably lack intellectual allure.

The sheer seductiveness of possibilities like those projected for virtual reality, we are convinced, plays as great a role in speculations on the future of computing as it does in our beliefs about Loch Ness. Delving through the literature of public commentary on computing, one quickly becomes accustomed to the reflexive use of terms like *revolutionary* and *millennial*. Views of computerization in these terms are simply so intriguing as to deaden many a reader's critical faculties. Consider a notable early work, the late Christopher Evans' *The Micro-Millennium*. Writing in 1979, Evans took a stance that was partly visionary, partly missionary:

> As with the Industrial Revolution...[the computer revolution] will have an overwhelming and comprehensive impact, affecting every human being on earth in every aspect of his or her life. Again, paralleling its predecessor, it will run at a gallop, though its time course will be shorter and its force may well be spent not in 150 years, but in twenty-five. Thirdly—again note the parallel—once the Revolution is under way it will be unstoppable, for reasons which we will consider in detail. (p. 11, from the Introduction.)

Evans did not restrict himself to generalities; his book is replete with concrete predictions. Consider his confident words on the incorporation of intelligent "sensors" in cars, and the consequent obsolescence of auto theft.

> By the late 1980's, these sensors could be standard, or even compulsory, equipment in all cars, together with other safety monitors such as microprocessors which monitor tyre wear, brake power, steering alignment and so on. They may even have the capacity to disconnect the car's electrical system if they "think" that any of its mechanical systems are in a dangerous state. A car which refuses to start when its driver has ingested too much alcohol has often been joked about, but it could well be the only type on the road in the late 1980's. By then most cars will be virtually theft-proof... (pp. 134-35)

Evans was hardly naive; indeed, his commentaries are often acutely perceptive of possibilities implicit in the technology. But by the time he wrote, a kind of speculative bubble in pronouncements on computing had already taken shape. In this process, commentators bid against one another to propound the most striking, most mind-boggling statements on what could be expected from the technologies. The result, inevitably, is a steady rise in the ante of speculation, and a relaxation of critical judgment on such possibilities.

Under such conditions, one wins few readers or listeners by suggesting that the social repercussions of the new technologies may be a good deal more complex, and much more muted, than others are willing to entertain. As with the Loch Ness monster, speculation becomes an enticing end in itself. In the case of computing, no one can expect to turn many heads by suggesting that its future social role may well prove far less flamboyant and more nuanced than the most eye-catching commentaries have suggested.

Thus, in a much-noted work published in 1988, Shoshana Zuboff spun an intoxicating vision of the dangers and possibilities posed by computing in the workplace. Citing a term already over-applied to the technology at the time, she wrote:

> Information technology is frequently hailed as "revolutionary." What are the implications of this term?... The informating capacity of the new computer-based technologies brings about radical change as it alters the intrinsic character of work—the way millions of people experience daily life on the job. It also poses fundamentally new choices for our organizational futures, and the ways in which labor and management respond to these new choices will finally determine whether our era becomes a time for radical change or a return to the familiar patterns and pitfalls of the traditional workplace. An emphasis on the informating capacity of intelligent technology can provide a point of origin for new conceptions of work and power. A more restricted emphasis on its automating capacity can provide the occasion for that second kind of revolution—a return to the familiar grounds of industrial society with divergent interests battling for control... (pp. 11-12)

We hardly doubt the authenticity of the observations presented by Zuboff from her own investigations. We do wonder, though, about *how typical* the effects that she posits may be. Whether the sweeping, computer-generated transformations that she notes are in store for rank-and-file organizations like those we have studied is hardly self-evident. In a realm as vast and multifarious as computing, almost any development can probably be documented in one setting or another. Reliable judgments of what constitutes standard or typical experience with computing, however, are much more problematic.

Zuboff apparently was not much troubled by concerns like these. "There is ample evidence," she writes, "to suggest that these plants are highly representative among manufacturing organizations in the manner that they have chosen to interpret new information technology" (1988, p. 283). But it is hard to know what such evidence might consist of. In relation to the organizations we have studied, Zuboff's cases of computer innovation appear to us notably flamboyant, showy and extreme. It is as if a botanist were documenting features of orchids that had been developed by selective breeding in hothouse environments. The results would not necessarily constitute good preparation for the study of native species in wild settings.

Our Approach

"Don't sell the steak," goes some famous advice to advertising copywriters; "sell the sizzle." Most writers on computing have found this insight impossible to resist, and with a subject like this, there is a lot of "sizzle" to sell. Under these circumstances, it is hardly surprising that the widest attention attaches to the best-told tales, rather than to the most balanced judgments.

The highly-charged valences of meaning projected in the public mythology of computing have not always made it easy to study the phenomena. Much of the difficulty has to do with the countless interpretations of the "potentials" of information technologies for social transformation. We hardly doubt that computing has the potentials ascribed to it in the writings of Zuboff and other enthusiastic commentators. The problem is that this is a technology whose potentials are endlessly multifarious. The devil of interpretation lies in the detail: *which particular* potentials are apt to be predominate in the broad sweep of social change? It will not do, we suggest, to assume that the answer lies in the most eye-catching or obviously "futuristic" possibilities. The most intriguing possibilities may simply not presage what is to follow.

For this reason, the research reported here takes what might be considered the opposite approach from that adopted by Zuboff and many other commentators. We have focused on the full range of computing activities reported in a representative sample of quite ordinary private-sector organizations. From the mid-1980s to the 1990s, we followed the evolution of computing in these establishments, aiming above all to record the main uses to which computing was put. At the same time, we have documented a number of other key indices of the social and economic state of these organizations, including changes in staffing, revenue, and management structure.

Note that what qualified establishments for inclusion in our survey was reliance on computing *in any form*. Thus we have sought to view the full range of uses of this multifarious technology as actually employed in typical organizations. Not surprisingly, the computing applications caught in this comprehensive net were quite heterogeneous—from computerized machine tools in manufacturing firms to computerized ordering systems in restaurants. Some few of these turned out to be highly sophisticated, eye-catching routines that would have won attention from writers like Evans or Zuboff. But most had little of such razzle-dazzle appeal. Most, in fact, proved to be relatively straightforward electronic versions of conventional activities. This is hardly to deny that their presence may hold much significance for the future of the organizations involved. But specifying that significance is not a simple task.

The reader can think of the accounts on which the following analyses are based, then, as something like a series of unretouched snapshots. These glimpses disclose standard uses of computing in private-sector organizations, at a point where the technology was just making the transformation from the exotic to the commonplace. They are drawn from interviews with decision-makers in our mostly rather ordinary organizations—figures who saw themselves not as visionaries, but as practical people struggling with day-to-day exigencies of work in their establishments.

In the pages to follow, we juxtapose the results of these interviews against the prevailing images of computerization derived from the literature. Our approach is inductive and skeptical. After sketching how the study was carried out (Chapter 2), we begin by examining the purposes for which computing was adopted in these organizations, and the evolution of those purposes over time (Chapter 3). We then examine the role of computing in the supervision of work, and its role in changing efficiency and employment levels in these organizations (Chapters 4 and 5). Finally, in the concluding chapters (6 and 7), we consider changes in the formal structure of organizations that appear to have ensued from computerization, and the longer-term changes in the character of organizational action that may be expected as computerization evolves over the next decades.

Part of our aim here is a critique of prevailing intellectual strategies in the study of computing. Specifically, we warn against the single-minded pursuit of unique "computing effects" across arrays of settings as heterogeneous as those studied here. With the exception of clerical workers, our own sample generally shows minimal net "effects" on the distribution of staff across job categories. But such findings should hardly represent the last word on the relationships involved. Within specific establishments, our interviews make it plain that specific computing innovations often have dramatic effects. That is, specific computing applications will generate or eliminate specific jobs, or reduce or increase specific costs. But the direction and extent of such effects remains highly contextual. Quite different consequences may result from the introduction of "the same" technology in apparently similar organizations. The fact that such different effects may cancel each other statistically should hardly deflect our interest in the underlying processes.

Fortunately, the design of our study affords the possibility of both statistical analyses and detailed looks at individual cases. By juxtaposing analysis of statistics on these organizations with accounts of specific processes, events, and attitudes within specific establishments, we hoped to achieve a more complete vision of the underlying reality. Where other commentators have offered categorical predictions of revolutionary "effects" of computing in transforming organizations, our statistics often provide legitimate grounds for reevaluating such expectations. And where context matters in shaping the role played by computing in the life of the organization, the detail of our site interviews can often show *how* it matters.

* * *

We are convinced that computing, unlike the Loch Ness Monster, represents an authentic force for social change. Part of that force is clearly bound up with its associated mythology. Unfortunately, that mythology has not always made it easy to chart the character of this force. Our purpose here is to understand that mythology, and to wear away a bit at its effects, by confronting mythic ideas with empirical insights from the grassroots of computer assimilation. To this end, we ask the reader to share our skepticism of the prevailing mythology, without rejecting those ideas outright. By examining the fine detail of the actual workings of computing in everyday organizations, we believe that both the value and the limitations of the mythic ideas surrounding the technology will become apparent.

2

The New York Study: Design and Execution

Early in the 1980s, Paul Attewell and James Rule, then colleagues in sociology at the State University of New York at Stony Brook, found themselves absorbed in dialogue over many of the issues raised in the preceding chapter. The discussions kept coming back to a single point: that research on computing had concentrated on dazzling possibilities and flamboyant case studies, at the expense of attention to the typical and widespread realities of computing practice. Over a period of months, we considered how new research might redress this situation. Ultimately, we sought and obtained funding from the National Science Foundation for a pilot study of these issues.

At the beginning of the pilot study, we were more certain of which features of earlier research we wanted to avoid than of which steps to take in our own right. We did know that we wanted to focus on the role of computing in *organizations*, preferably the widest possible variety of them. Of course, we wanted to develop some form of sampling design that would focus, as much as possible, on the full array of computer-using organizations. For similar reasons, we wanted to avoid an exclusive association of "computing" with any one use of the multifarious technology. In other words, we did not want just to study computerized financial operations, or production control, or strategic planning. Instead, we wanted to begin the investigation with something as close as possible to a *census* of computing activities, across a representative selection of organizations. Only by casting such a wide and inclusive net could we end up in a position to generalize about the full range of roles played by the technology. Finally, we wanted to make our inquiries to some degree *historical*. That is, we wanted to seek data on the timing and

15

sequence of computing adoption, in juxtaposition with other important events in the evolution of the organizations under study.

The Pilot Interviews

We approached the pilot study inductively. We began simply by contacting organizations known by us to use computing in one way or another, and requesting the chance to visit the site and conduct an interview. Out of these initially unstructured encounters, we began to get a sense of the range of computer activities that we would need to address, and to frame an interview that would do justice to the variety of these phenomena.

One lesson immediately learned from these encounters was that "computing" was normally not a single, coherent activity in most of the organizations we visited. Organizations, it was apparent, used very different forms of computing for different purposes. Perhaps unsurprisingly, these different activities had varying salience for the people concerned. Some were regarded as innovative and distinctive by those we interviewed, whereas others were hardly noticed as anything special. For such reasons, effort was often required to get our interlocutors to identify *all* elements of their work that involved computing. On more than one occasion, pilot interviewers had virtually completed their conversations on the "computing" in use at a particular site—only to learn at the last minute of computerized activities that had not been brought to their attention. Thus, in a manufacturing company, a vice-president concerned with computerized accounting procedures might spend hours describing these activities to us—while inadvertently failing to mention the computerized machine tools in use on the shop floor.

Evidently any one organization was apt to have quite distinct stories to tell about the various computing activities in use at the site. Clearly separate data intakes would be necessary for each distinct computer *application*—each separate "bundle" of activities carried out by computer processes at the site.

Evolution of the 1985 Interview

From the earliest stages, then, our interview evolved in bipartite form. The initial portion sought information about the establishment as a whole—its history, the products or services it produced, staffing levels, and the like. But the second part of each interview aimed to document each individual application in use at the site. This routine was repeated separately for each application so identified. Thus, in a large, highly computerized organization, the interviewer might find himself repeating the same routine of questions for a computerized payroll system, a computerized inventory control system, a word processing system and, perhaps, several other applications.

How, then, were we to reckon what counted as a distinct application? This question raised problems both conceptual and practical. Computing activities within any organization have a way of blending into one another. Often a single computer may be used to do quite different things. Elsewhere, what might be considered the "same" computing activities are carried out on a variety of different machines. After many false starts, we ultimately designated an application as a set of computerized activities that (1) rely on distinct software and (2) run off their own data base. Thus, a system that maintained inventories of finished goods and performed sales analyses based on these same data would be regarded as representing a single application, so long as the same software was involved. If different software programs used the same data base for different purposes, we would classify the arrangement as constituting two distinct applications.

Consider payroll preparation. It is very common for organizations to computerize this activity, using either off-the-shelf or customized software. Data for payroll purposes are entered from personnel records and elsewhere in the organization; using these data in conjunction with information of hours worked, deductions, and the like makes it possible to generate both payroll checks and records of past payrolls. We normally counted such payroll routines as constituting distinct applications—except for rare cases where such activities seemed to blend indistinguishably into other financial operations.

By the same token, many establishments relied on computing for inventory control—for keeping track of raw materials, finished products, or both. These we usually also bracketed as distinct applications, but here, too, boundaries were sometimes not so clear-cut. Some computerized inventory routines, for example, operated in conjunction with systems that also entered work orders and recorded their completion. If the same system was both keeping track of raw materials used in production and recording the shipment of finished products, we regarded it as a single, inclusive application.

The need to treat each distinct application separately placed special demands on the interviewers. Each interview began with our routine of questions on the establishment as a whole. By the end of this first portion of the interview, however, the interviewer needed to have identified the various applications that were the focus for the second part of the interview. Here the same inquiries were repeated for each separate application, including questions on the purposes served by the application, the date of its inception, the roles of those who used the application, its implications for staffing, and a variety of other issues. In organizations with many applications, the many iterations of this portion of the interview could require hours. Often interviewers found it necessary to direct inquiries about different applications to different informants within the establishment.

In general, the first part of the interview furnished data for background variables on the establishments under study. The second, iterative part covering each distinct application provided most of the information we needed on computing activities. Moreover, the *number* of applications recorded within each establishment provided, as we note below, a key index of the extent of computerization.

Much of the data collected in both parts of the interview was obviously highly objective and circumscribed. For such matters as the number of persons employed at a particular site, or the functions served by specific computing applications, the interview relied on terse, survey-like questions. But we also sought as much as possible to make a place in the interview for less structured exchanges between interviewer and interlocutor, more in the mode of ethnographic or field interviewing. Each interview schedule thus contained instructions from probes like, "Has the existence of...this application led to a search for new ways of using this capability? If yes, explain. Has search been successful?" (1985 interview, Part II, item 19). Opportunities to pursue such lines of questioning could hardly be taken for granted, given that many busy interlocutors insisted on concluding the interviews as rapidly as possible. But where rapport was good and time not too short, interviewers had the chance not only to pursue less structured lines of questioning, but also to observe work routines and to speak informally with staff. At the end of each interview, moreover, interviewers also encouraged those who had answered the survey-like questions to comment broadly on the role of computing in their organizations. These informal exchanges also yielded much suggestive supplementary information.

In writing up their work, interviewers used a standard template for recording data from Parts I and II—data on the establishment as a whole, and the separate iterations of data recorded for each application. In addition, each interviewer set down one or more paragraphs of summary—discursive commentary on his over-all impressions of computing at the site. Often these non-standard comments proved useful in our subsequent analyses of the data and in our decisions as to which establishments to choose for further visits.

A complete example of the interview form ultimately adopted is found in Appendix 7.1 below.

Sampling

On the strength of the results of the pilot study, the National Science Foundation provided funding for a full-scale survey of computer use. Thus we began a period of intensive interviewing and data analysis lasting from 1985 to 1989.

We sought above all to develop a portrait of computer use in a set of organizations that would be statistically representative. Ideally, we would have preferred to generalize about computing activities throughout all organizations in America. This proved to be a utopian aspiration. Organizations that rely on computing, after all, come in the greatest variety—from the CIA to the United Fund to the corner grocery. To choose a representative sample, we needed to locate something like an exhaustive *list* of some well-delineated category of organizations. We were sure that no one had created a list of *all* computer-using organizations. The problem was to find the most comprehensive list available for sampling.

After some concerted searching, we located a list developed by a market research firm that fulfilled many of our requirements. This was a list of private-sector organizations in greater New York that were known to have purchased computing equipment. It contained much background information on the organizations listed, including size, location, and other data of interest to us. The company that had created this list was willing, for a price, to draw a stratified random sample from it.

This source was not ideal. For one thing, it contained no government organizations, which held as much interest for us as those in the private sector. But it did cover organizations of all sizes and from all industrial sectors, including some non-profit organizations. Another disadvantage was that this list contained no *un*computerized organizations that might have provided a control group for our computerized cases. This was a matter of some discussion and concern. In many ways, we would have preferred to study the workings of computerized organizations in parallel to similar establishments *not* relying on computing. Any such control group, however, would have been a volatile asset in that non-computerized organizations were well on their way to being converted to the computerized category at the time of our study.

On the other hand, a particular advantage of this list was the detail of information it held on each organization. This made it easy to *stratify* our sample—to choose organizations from specific subcategories within the large sample so as to ensure that the establishments we ultimately interviewed would be as varied as possible. Accordingly, we specified a sample stratified along the following four dimensions:

(1) *extent of computerization within organizations:* two levels.

(2) *region within the New York area:* three sub-regions: Manhattan; Brooklyn and Queens; and the two suburban counties of Long Island.

(3) *industrial category:* ten Standard Industrial Classification (SIC) categories.

(4) *size, in terms of numbers of employees:* three categories, in terms of numbers employed at the establishment where the interview took place: those with 30 or fewer staff; those with 31 to 100 staff; and those with 101 or more.

In each case, we charged the market research firm to sample equal, or nearly equal, numbers of cases from each of the subcategories mentioned above.

As it turned out, the interviewing team was assembled and ready to begin in the autumn of 1985, some weeks before the market researchers could complete drawing the sample. In order not to delay the beginning of the research, we began by selecting for interview some twenty-five organizations from the greater New York business-to-business telephone directory. The distribution of these organizations on key variables largely parallels that of the rest of our sample, as Table 2.1 demonstrates. For more detailed comparison of these twenty-five cases with the statistically-drawn sample, please see Appendix 2.1.

As Table 2.1 shows, some 161 of the 200 organizations in our stratified, random sample ultimately provided interviews, for a response rate of 80.5 percent. Added to the twenty-five interviews with firms selected from the telephone directory, this yielded a total of 186 completed interviews.

Table 2.1

Origins of Sample 1985 (n=186).

Standard Industrial Classification		Size of Establishment			
		Small	Medium	Large	*TOTAL*
Discrete Manufacturing	Phone Book	4	2	2	*8*
	Research Sample	4	3	6	*13*
Durable Wholesale	Phone Book	0	0	1	*1*
	Research Sample	7	7	2	*16*
Finance/ Real Estate/ Insurance	Phone Book	0	0	0	*0*
	Research Sample	6	3	6	*15*
Services	Phone Book	2	1	2	*5*
	Research Sample	6	7	8	*21*
Construction	Phone Book	0	0	0	*0*
	Research Sample	3	3	6	*12*
Non-Durable Wholesale	Phone Book	2	0	1	*3*
	Research Sample	6	7	5	*18*
Process Manufacturing	Phone Book	3	1	1	*5*
	Research Sample	7	3	8	*18*
Retail	Phone Book	0	2	0	*2*
	Research Sample	10	5	6	*21*
Transport/ Communic/ Utilities	Phone Book	0	1	0	*1*
	Research Sample	7	4	7	*18*
Other	Phone Book	0	0	0	*0*
	Research Sample	5	1	3	*9*
Total Establishments	Phone Book	11	7	7	*25*
	Research Sample	61	43	57	*161*
	Total	72	50	64	*186*

The 1985 Interviews

As we began the interviewing, we hired a dedicated office manager who would act as our scheduler. Her role was to contact organizations from the sample, beseech their participation in the study, and schedule, re-schedule, and (when necessary) re-re-schedule interviews with the utmost tenacity. Over a period of more than twelve months of interviewing, her efforts succeeded in producing the respectable response rates cited above.

No less critical were the services of two highly qualified full-time interviewers, Kevin Delaney and Steven Cohen, who each ultimately devoted more than a year of their careers to the study. Both these young men had doctoral training in sociology, and both brought analytical insight as well as energy and concentration to the work. Their duties required that they travel considerable distances to interviews, from Manhattan, where the project had its headquarters, to the distant reaches of Long Island, nearly one hundred miles away.

Thus the research team consisted of two principal investigators—Paul Attewell and James Rule—and the three just mentioned. As the interviewing unfolded, we constituted ourselves as a kind of occasional seminar, carrying out a continuing internal critique of the work. We sought to judge strengths and weaknesses of specific interviews, noting patterns that seemed to be emerging, and making occasional mid-course changes in the interview design.

Throughout the study, our unit of analysis was the *establishment*, rather than the entire company. This distinction needed to be considered in some 44.6% (83) of the 186 cases from our 1985 sample, where the establishment that we visited was not the only location of the organization concerned. In these instances, interviewers were instructed to record data on matters like sales activity and corporate ownership—questions that could only apply to the company as a whole. But queries on matters such as employment levels and computing practices focused strictly on the single site.

In setting up the interviews, it was not always easy to know who at the site would make the best informant. Usually we had to satisfy ourselves with the self-selection of the person willing to designate him or herself as the appropriate figure to talk to us. In bigger establishments, this might be the management information systems director, or a vice-president responsible for data processing. In smaller settings, our interlocutors were often the owner or general manager.

In some larger organizations, a number of different informants relayed each other, as the interviewer was passed from one interlocutor to another. Often these occasions seemed to yield the best interviews.

Interviewing began in September 1985 and continued into early 1987. The routine was often stressful, given the far-flung geographical dispersion of interview sites and the difficulty of securing firm appointments for interviews. Despite the scheduler's best efforts, interviewers would often spend hours traveling to a site, only to be told that the person who had agreed to the interview was unable to see them. On a number of occasions, interviewers returned several times before completing their work.

Interviews ranged from at least an hour to marathon sessions spread over several visits. It was by no means unusual for a single interview to last all day, leaving all parties exhausted. The length of interviews varied directly with the size of the organization. Bigger organizations generally reported having begun computing earlier and doing more of it. Accordingly, they had longer, more complex stories to tell, with more applications to describe, and more people involved in telling about them.

There was much variation in the rapport and richness of interviews. In many cases, the interviewers considered themselves lucky if their interlocutor would sit still long enough to answer the bare minimum of survey-type questions. In other organizations, large and small, informants willingly continued to talk well after the formal parts of the interviews were completed. These latter conversations were enormously valuable, affording all sorts of insights and reflections that could never have been obtained by direct questioning.

On returning from interviews, the interviewers spent hours recording the results of their inquiries. For this purpose, we designed an electronic template, so that responses to the survey-like questions could be entered quickly. In addition to these more structured bits of data entry, the interviewers also provided their discursive overview of their impressions of the state of computing at each site. These typically included observations on unforeseen or idiosyncratic aspects of computing use at the establishment in question.

Once recorded, every interview was in turn reviewed by one of the principal investigators, and often revised and amplified in light of these readings. Completed interviews were then coded and stored electronically.

The 1993 Interviews

By the early 1990s, the results of these interviews had been published in a number of studies (Attewell and Rule 1984; Rule and Attewell 1989; Rule 1991; Rule and Brantley 1992). As computing continued to attract attention from researchers, and from the public more generally, we could not help wondering how the technology was evolving in the organizations we had surveyed in the mid-1980s. Had these establishments continued to computerize? How had the process of computerization interacted with broader economic changes in the greater New York business climate during this period? This latter question took on special interest, given that the boom conditions prevailing during the first wave of interviews had given rise to a stubborn economic recession by the beginning of the 1990s. Above all: what had become of the specific applications we saw in place, or being put in place, in the mid-1980s? Would decision-makers continue to feel that their use was justified? What changes would have occurred in the ways these applications were used? Would any have triggered, for example, the "revolutionary" changes envisaged by some commentators?

Consequently, we sought a new round of interviews with these same organizations, creating a panel study of change over time. The second wave of interviews, also funded by the National Science Foundation, was somewhat less ambitious than the first. To avoid the complications of scheduling and carrying out site visits, these new interviews were mainly done by telephone. The aim was not to replicate every part of the first interview, but to parallel the more structured parts of that interview, at the expense of its more discursive aspects. The key aim was to chart how the use of computing had changed—which applications were now in use, for example, what role the original and new computing activities were playing within the life of the organization, and how these things related to over-all changes in the fortunes and activities of each organization.

The structure of the 1993 interview closely paralleled that of the survey-like aspects of the earlier one. Like the latter, the second-wave interviews began with questions about the state of the organization as a whole, as in Part I of the earlier interview. Special attention was paid to changes in the economic fortunes of the organization since the earlier interview, as well as to any other qualitative and quantitative changes that might affect its reliance on computing. How, we wanted to know, had the organization fared in the recession that began at the end of the 1980s? Was it still producing the same sorts of goods and services as at the time of the earlier interview? What new computing equipment had been acquired since then?

As in the earlier study, the second-wave interviews were largely given over to detailing specific computing applications. For each application identified in the first-wave interviews, the second-wave interviewer sought to update our information. Was the application still in existence? How had it been altered, if at all? What workers were now involved in its operation? Had anyone been dismissed or transferred because of it? And of course, we sought information on new applications adopted since the first interviews. The full text of the 1993 interview can be found in Appendix 7.2.

As in the original interviews, response rate was a key concern. In 1993 and 1994, we re-contacted 146 firms from our earlier sample. The other forty had either gone our of business (as attested by a credit reporting company), moved out of New York state, changed their names, or for other reasons could not be contacted. Of the 146 remaining firms, forty-eight either refused or were unavailable for interview. In the remaining ninety-eight cases, a telephone interview was carried out, with, wherever possible, the same person who provided the 1985 interview.

In sixteen of those ninety-eight cases, the telephone interview revealed that the establishment had undergone some form of what we judged to be drastic exogenous change since the previous interview. Such changes mostly consisted of acquisition by, or a merger with, an outside company. In these cases, we did not feel confident in assuming that we were dealing with the "same" establishment that we had interviewed in the 1980s. Accordingly, these sixteen organizations are excluded from most of the statistical analyses presented below, so that our final panel consists of eighty-two establishments.

Table 2.2 shows the numbers of organizations and applications covered in the two phases of the study.

As Table 2.2 shows, some 47.3% (88/186) of the organizations we interviewed in 1985 were unavailable for interview in 1993. But both these 1985 interviews and those of organizations deemed to have undergone drastic exogenous change by 1993 provide case study material for discussion below.

Table 2.2

Sample and Applications 1985 and 1993.

	1985 All	1985 Panel	1993 All	1993 Panel
Number of Organizations	186	82	98	82
Number of Applications	541	230	422	351
Applications per Organization	2.9	2.8	4.3	4.3

Conclusion

The two-stage interviewing process thus ultimately yielded what we had originally sought—a pair of "censuses" of computing activities in a representative group of organizations. One could think of this census as a pair of snapshots taken at points when the technology was just making the transition from being a specialty mainly of larger, more sophisticated organizations to being a normal feature of most private-sector organizations. These snapshots documented above all the purposes served by computing applications and the adaptations made to these applications over time. They also recorded the perceptions of managers and planners in these organizations as to the role computing had played in them thus far, and further computer developments in the offing.

We should also note the limitations of these interviews. In the effort to secure comparable data on a large, statistically generalizable sample, we created an interview that rarely afforded extended field observation in any organization. To put matters less formally: we rarely got to "hang out" at length in the establishments we visited. For the most part, we had to rely on the words of management informants. Therefore, we could rarely gather direct data on perceptions or attitudes of lower-level workers toward computerization. For similar reasons, we seldom had the opportunity to observe computerized work long enough to judge for ourselves whether the systems operated in practice in the ways our management informants claimed that they did. True, a few interviews marked by especially good rapport did yield opportunities for the interviewers to develop such insights. But for the most part, depth of attention to any single organization was sacrificed in the interest of making parallel inquiries in a varied and representative array of computerized settings.

We did create one opportunity to countervail against these limitations. At the end of the 1993 interviews, Debra Gimlin and James Rule reviewed their results and identified a number of organizations that appeared to have particularly interesting stories to tell, if only we could return for longer, unstructured interviews. After extensive appeals, we did in fact carry out roughly twenty leisurely, discursive visits to these establishments—considerably enriching our understanding of the changes taking place in the panel organizations. Here we could inquire in much fuller detail why crucial computerization decisions were taken, and how these decisions had worked out in practice. Information from these interviews forms the basis for many of the following discussions.

Appendix 2.1

Statistical Tests Comparing Phone Book Sample with Market Research Sample (N=186).

1985 Firm Characteristics	Random Sample Selected From Phone Book (N=25)		Random Sample Selected by Market Research Firm (N=161)		Analysis	
	Mean	SD	Mean	SD	t	p
Age of Firm (Years)[a]	61.6	31.2	46.0	24.7	2.40	0.024
Size of Firm (Total # Employees)	104.8	199.9	100.0	122.1	0.12	ns
Number of Months Computing	50.2	40.0	61.9	53.2	-1.06	ns
Total Number of Checklist Items	11.0	7.0	8.8	5.3	1.87	ns
Total Number of Applications	2.6	1.5	3.0	1.6	-1.20	ns

[a] One organization missing due to missing response on year firm founded.

ns: Not statistically significant.

3

What Computers Do;
How Computing Changes

[215]* is located on the West Side of midtown Manhattan, amid the loft buildings and loading docks that crowd next to the Hudson. This small business specializes in construction of a rather specialized sort: installation of the "dropped" ceilings used ubiquitously in office buildings and elsewhere to conceal wiring, plumbing and other architectural necessities. At the time of our first interview in 1986, this privately owned company employed about 125, roughly half of whom were carpenters and others physically engaged in the installation. At that point, the level of computerization prevailing in [215] was just barely enough to qualify it for inclusion our sample: it consisted of one accounting application.

Consider how that application came to be adopted. Around 1980, our interviewer reported, management grew dissatisfied with its collections. The company was simply not receiving payment from its customers as fast as it should, and efforts to collect were taking too much staff time.

Part of the problem stemmed from certain special features of the company's business. As the interviewer explained in his original notes, billings by this company involve a lot of "extras"

> or additional tasks which are not mentioned in the original contract which must be billed as separate jobs. So, for example, a job may be won at the Empire State Building and a contract drawn up with monthly requisitions of $25,000 for a period of 14 months. During this period...there may be 25 extra things done in the first month, 6 done in the second month, none done in the third month, and so forth. Each of these "extras" must be given a job number and billed as a separate job order.

---

* To preserve the confidentiality of the organizations that contributed to our study, we substituted numbers for their names.

29

The time-consuming, labor-intensive nature of these billing processes, it was felt, represented an appealing target for some form of computerization. In particular, the right system would make it possible to enter the basic facts on each job once, with additional entries for each "extra"—and to have bills to each contractor generated automatically regularly thereafter, until they were paid. Such a system would "flag" late accounts so that staff could devote special attention to getting them paid.

In 1986, after years of deliberation, the company put into place a system of this kind. Cautiously, managers ran the new computing arrangements in parallel with their conventional, paper-based system for three months, before entrusting their billing completely to it. At the time of our first interview, some three months after that, the manager supervising accounting operations pronounced himself satisfied with the results. With the new system, in the words of our interviewer,

> there is more time for the workers to handle a greater volume of work...there is more accurate calculation of charges than before, there is less direct supervision of workers than before, and, for the collections workers, there is more time spent on actually tracking down customers and less time spent on looking up information about jobs in the files...the [collections] clerk doesn't have to spend much time going to the files to look up the name or phone number of the person at a particular job site responsible for paying [215]...[so that this person can] "stay on the phone and out of the files", as [the informant] put it.

When this first interview took place, management was contemplating extending this cautious first step to include computerization of all its accounting activities.

The Functions of Computing

In a body of cases as heterogeneous as ours, it would be oversimplified to single out any one organization or application as "typical." But this story from [215] presents features that we encountered again and again throughout the study. Decision-makers, reacting to a bottleneck in the flow of work or some other frustrating circumstance, conceive the idea that some form of computerization could provide an answer. In a minority of cases—some 11 percent of the all computing applications reported in 1985—such steps are actively promoted by outsiders to the organization, such as computer vendors or consultants. But most often, informants report that decisions to computerize stemmed most directly from considerations arising within the ownership or management of the organization.

Consider another adoption story no less typical than the one noted above. This was a text-management application developed by [145], a suburban retailer of forklift vehicles, with twenty-seven staff in 1985. This company faced a recurrent bottleneck in drawing up the complex contracts that it proposed to its customers. Since each forklift ordered was to some degree customized for a specific use, blocks of nearly-identical legal "boilerplate" had to be interspersed with specific descriptions of specific forklifts. In the words of the interviewer,

> In the past, the salesman would return to the office with several pages of specifications—like the height that the fork must be able to [reach]...the length of the forks and so on—and the secretaries would have to type them up. These quotations often run three or more pages...[and] the company does about 100 or so of these a week, a job which could easily occupy all the time of a single person... [This application formats] the standard kinds of forklifts and also provides space for all the possible kinds of special adaptation these standard types can accommodate. In addition, this computerized quotation formats a standard contract either for a lease or for a sale, thus further simplifying the paper work involved in getting from the sale and salesman to the customer's decision to buy. They are printed up in triplicate...

The interviewer comments,

> the salesmen have a much easier time responding to the demands of their customers...with this quotations application, because changes can be made easily and paperwork bottlenecks have been eliminated.

This excerpt also illustrates another recurrent characteristic of applications documented in our sample—their marked continuity with activities already established within the organization. As conceived by decision-makers, and as initially executed, this application simply duplicated what the secretarial staff had done, though the execution was obviously quicker. Like the billing program instated by [215], this instance of computerization could hardly be described as "revolutionary" in relation to the established agenda of the organization. Instead, like the vast majority of all applications documented in this study, these two represented incremental changes in means for accomplishing ends long pursued in these organizations. Comprehensive computerization programs that involve sweeping changes of work objectives or conceptual frames are rarely if ever found in our sample.

Much the same can be said for the steps taken by a third organization from our sample [107], a retailer of rebuilt auto parts, to computerize its inventory. In addition to selling its own salvaged and rebuilt items, this small company fills customer orders with parts purchased from other suppliers. The need to keep track of such vast numbers of discrete units must have made the attractions of computerization obvious. In the words of the interviewer in 1985,

> when junk is brought into the shop...it is taken apart and numbered. All such information must go into the inventory file. All of the GM, Ford and Lucas parts information must...[also be inventoried]. The numbered parts from the junk heap are then worked on in the shop, where they are re-built into saleable parts, which too must be numbered, packaged and stocked. If one includes its on-site inventory from the major companies, its own re-built parts, and the national inventories of the major producers...[the total comes to] nearly a million inventory items.

According to this report, the comprehensive inventory system took two full-time clerical workers some seven months to enter. The result was a system that provided quick information as to what was in stock; when items being sought proved not to be in stock, they could be ordered directly by computer from other sources.

Very commonly, in our sample, computerization simply furthered the evolution of refinements that had long been under way via conventional technologies. This was the case in with a fourth application—a relatively complex, sophisticated routine developed by [238], a suburban printing company that produces advertising and discount coupons and employs about 520. [238] had developed what it called its "job jacket" application as a means for following the evolution of each distinct printing order from start to finish. In the words of the interviewer,

> The application is used first by customer service representatives [who enter]...what type and size of paper the customer wants, what size the ad should be, the colors and art to be used. These features are entered into the computer in something akin to a grid format. From here, the Scheduling Department determines an appropriate time frame for the job. The Prep Supervisor uses...[this application] to assess the requirements of the job; he produces the film necessary for it. After that, the Plate Supervisor uses the job jacket for instructions on how he should create the plate for the actual run and the Binding Supervisor gets instructions for the binding of the job. At each stop along the way, workers must enter into the system the amount of time they spent on the project, which is later used for billing purposes. After the Binding Supervisor, the job jacket returns to the Customer Service Representative who okays the job with the client before the actual run. The system then produces a "request for billing" that goes to the Cost Accounting Department and then finally to the Billing Department where the invoice is produced via word processor.

Note that certain features of the "job jacket" application replicate those of the accounting program developed by [215]:

Now, the job jacket keeps track of..."Author Alterations," or changes the clients request after a job was begun... When the job jacket was kept manually, these changes were frequently made but rarely charged to the client. By including these alterations in billing, the firm brings in an estimated $22,000 per year.

Before the job jacket application was a computer program, it was a physical dossier, an actual jacket of notes and specifications on work orders. Clearly the role of computing in this case has been to abet and enhance an activity that had always been central to the work of this and other printing companies. This state of affairs is the rule among our cases.

Standardization of Computing Functions

From one perspective, each of these four applications may appear utterly particular to the organizations that adopted them. But once the study was under way, it quickly became apparent that a relative handful of basic *genres* of computing activity were being replicated across a wide variety of organizational settings. In fact, each of the four applications described above is emblematic of a major category of computing activity that is represented widely throughout our sample. These basic application types do four things: (1) they *maintain accounts* as in the billing application adopted by [215], or as in applications that generate payrolls or sales analyses; (2) they *store and manage text* through one or another form of word processing, as in the contract-generating application developed by [145]; (3) they *enter work orders* and, in some cases, track work on those orders through their gestation within the organization, as in the "job jacket" program at [238]; or (4) they *monitor inventory*, either that of raw materials or finished products or both, as at [107].

Table 3.1 shows the distribution of these four basic computing functions among all applications reported by organizations in our study.

The three columns of percentages in Table 3.1 describe the three categories of data in the study. The first column consists of figures describing all organizations in the original 1985 sample of some 186 establishments; the second column consists of figures from 1985 interviews with 82 organizations that later also participated in the 1993 interviews; the third column shows data from those 1993 interviews. Data summarized in the middle column, in other words, are a subset of the data shown in column one.

Table 3.1

Distribution of Computing Functions Across All
Computing Applications, 1985 and 1993.

	1985 All Organizations		1985 Panel Organizations		1993 Panel Organizations	
	N	%	N	%	N	%
Total Applications	541	100.0	230	100.0	351	100.0
Financial	265	49.0	111	48.3	152	43.3
Order Entry/Job Tracking	70	12.9	25	10.9	26	7.4
Text Management	88	16.3	42	18.3	83	23.7
Inventory	29	5.4	14	6.1	18	5.1
Other	89	16.5	38	16.5	72	20.5

Table 3.1 makes a simple point that deserves attention: *the great majority of all computer applications documented in our study are of one of the four basic types described above.* The most widespread and typical uses of computing, in other words, are not highly specific to the organizations in which they occur. Instead, computing, as we encounter it here, consists overwhelmingly of a standardized series of practices replicated across this diversely representative selection of private-sector organizations.

As Table 3.1 shows, the distribution of key computing functions was also remarkably stable over time. Both in 1985 and 1993, nearly half of all computing applications were devoted to some form of accounting activity, ranging from payroll preparation to accounts payable and receivable to the general ledger, or over-all balance-sheet of the company. The broad category of accounting activities were remarkably standardized in turn: both in the 1985 samples and in 1993, at least two-thirds of all the accounting applications were devoted to the following five functions: general ledger, accounts receivable, accounts payable, billing, or payroll preparation.

One further measure of the standardization of computer applications was the extent to which they ran on off-the-shelf software—the one-size-fits-all programs marketed for everything from word processing to tax preparation. In the 1993 interview, we asked whether each application ran on such software. In 54.4% of the 351 applications, the answer was affirmative. These figures differed somewhat according to the functions of the applications involved: for financial applications, some 50.0% ran on off-the-shelf programs;

for inventory control, the proportion was 33.3%; for text management, 78.3%; for order entry, 38.5%.

Not all applications involving standardized activities fall exclusively into just one of the four functional categories. It is very common for a single application to embody two or more of the four functions. Consider a computer routine reported by a fast-food restaurant from our sample—a system for reckoning each order as entered in the computerized cash registers. This application in effect relieved the counter staff of virtually any thinking or discretion in their work, by calculating the cost of each order and deducting the ingredients required for each hamburger, milkshake or other item from inventory. Additionally, this application served (in the words of the interviewer) to

> stop theft and discover wastage. When items are delivered (meat patties, buns, etc.), the quantities are entered on the computer. Each time an order is entered on the [computerized] cash registers, these quantities are reduced by the appropriate amounts. For example, a hamburger is ordered and punched in on the cash register. The computer automatically reduces [inventory by] one hamburger patty, one hamburger roll, 1/8 oz. onions, one pickle...

We classified the function of this application in the first instance as one of inventory control. In some respects it could also be considered an order entry and job-tracking system, since it follows specific orders through their gestation within the establishment. In fact, this symbiosis within this single application has parallels throughout our sample. *Mutatis mutandis*, the schema described above could describe systems from our sample devoted to keeping track of drugs used in veterinary clinics; or sheet metal in manufacturing plants; or bottles of wines and spirits in liquor shops. In a vast array of such cases, computers are devoted to tracking large numbers of discrete inventory items and—often—recording the details of their use within the organization as specific jobs progress. In some instances, these applications automatically generate shipping labels and bills on the production of finished goods.

One might well wonder about the extent of this predictability *across* the various organizations in our sample. Do different *kinds* of organizations, or those in different social settings, rely on different mixes of computing functions? Our initial expectation was that this would indeed be the case, especially given the efforts we had taken to create the most diverse possible sample of representative organizations. Surely, we felt, manufacturing industries would have different patterns of computing use from, say, medical care providers or retailers.

In fact, we found few differences of this kind. As the frequency distributions in Appendix 3.1 show, most of the four basic functions of computing are represented in most industrial groups. There are a few, unsurprising exceptions—for example, we find that inventory control applications are much more common in manufacturing and retailing than in construction and financial services. But all industrial sectors rely on financial applications, and by 1993 all sectors reported at least some reliance on word processing. The overall picture is one of computing as an increasingly pervasive adjunct for accomplishing a core of administrative tasks that are extremely standardized across establishments.

Non-Standard Applications

A rather small minority of applications—never more than twenty percent of all those reported at any point in our study—do not involve these standardized functions. Given that they are defined by their differentness, generalizations about this minority of applications are all but impossible. As one example of such an application, consider the following case from [139], a manufacturer of plastics. This company is highly computerized; at the time of the first interview, we counted some seven distinct applications. One of these is devoted to testing every batch of plastics that it produces.

Such tests used to be done manually, by technicians who would draw small samples of material, administer certain analyses, perform hand calculations, and steer the process accordingly. Now such analyses are done by computer. According to our informant, the computer

> keeps better control of the product because the computer program gives consistent solutions to the same problem. Before computers, each lab tech would plot a graph and decide what should be added and how much [of each ingredient in the batch being prepared] was required to bring an item to spec. Now they don't really have that discretion.

We can find no other case in our sample qualitatively comparable to the use of computing technology described here. Testing the hardness and other qualities of a finished manufacturing product in general, and plastics in particular, is a one-of-a-kind activity in this sample.

Not all such apparently *sui generis* applications have this "high tech" character. Consider another application developed by [238], the large printing company whose "job jacket" program was described above. In addition to that application, this company developed a sophisticated electronic database of potential customers, listed in terms of the nature of the business they do and the past experience of the company with them. In the words of the interviewer,

> The database includes the characteristics of potential clients and a history of the firm's dealings with them, including the dates of salespersons' visits to the firms, any estimates [238] has provided for them in the past, the possible reasons these estimates failed to acquire a potential job, and which competing firms got the contract [238] bid on...
>
> The listing includes mostly ad agencies, since these are the types of clients [238] deals with most frequently. The company collects agency names from various sources, including magazines, membership lists, and advertising publications. Prospects are not included in the database until after they have been "cold called" by a [238] telemarketer, who discerns whether or not the company might be interested in contracting with [238]. If this is the case, the potential customer is added to the data base and is either assigned to one of [238's] 40 salespeople...or put in a pool of prospects. (10 March 1996)

The fact that this application is built on off-the-shelf software that was commercially available suggests that other organizations do something at least somewhat similar. But we cannot identify any other application from the 351 in our 1993 sample that serves this purpose of monitoring and pinpointing potential sources of business.

Much the same would apply to the rest of our "non-standard" applications. They are virtually as various as the deliberately heterogeneous array of organizations in our sample. They include computerized devices for guiding machine tools in manufacturing companies; a computerized algorithm for determining rates charged by an insurance company; a device for scheduling pickups by a small private bus company, etc. These applications range from the sophisticated to the obvious, though we would judge that few are likely to leave the reader breathless in their subtlety. What strikes us most forcefully is that there are so few of them, in relation to the vast majority of such highly classifiable cases turned up in this study.

* * *

Let us enter an interim observation on the findings reported thus far. With a small minority of exceptions, most of the applications we have documented are straightforward extensions of practices and aims previously pursued through non-computerized means. They may—or possibly, may not—offer all sorts of advantages to the organizations adopting them. What most of them do *not* seem to foster is a radical break with earlier activities and mindsets. They are mostly conceived and adopted, at least in the first instance, as superior tools for accomplishing standard and familiar tasks. Moreover, most computing is highly standardized across organizations. More than eighty percent of all applications are devoted to highly predictable, standard activities that might be found in virtually any organization.

Change in Computing

Growth in reliance on computing may be incremental among our organizations, but it is also pervasive. When the second wave of panel interviews began in 1993, it immediately became apparent that the great majority of establishments had continued to find new ways to use the technology. Among the eighty-two panel cases, the mean number of distinct computing applications rose from 2.8 to 4.3. The average establishment had added 1.5 applications, and only one establishment recorded a net reduction in computer applications in use.

The total number of applications in use in any establishment, then, represents one of the two key indices of extent of computerization that we use throughout this work. The other is the total of a checklist of activities susceptible to computerization—ranging from payroll preparation to inventory control—reported to be computerized at each site. This multi-item inventory, shown as part if the interview schedules in Appendices 2.1 and 2.3, was developed inductively during the pilot study as we accumulated knowledge of the various ways in which computing might be used in the organizations we studied. Like the total number of applications, the total numbers of checklist items show marked growth over the period of the panel study. Table 3.2 shows these changes in our two computing variables.

Table 3.2

Growth in Computing, 1985 to 1993.					
	1985 Panel Organizations		1993 Panel Organizations		Change in Computing (1985-1993)
	Mean	SD	Mean	SD	Mean	SD
Applications	2.8	1.5	4.3	1.9	1.5	1.4
Checklist Items	8.2	4.7	13.9	7.0	5.7	5.6

SD: Standard Deviation

Our panel organizations, then, showed considerable growth in reliance on computing between 1985 and 1993. Figures 3.1 through 3.3 demonstrate this growth and its distribution across the four basic functions discussed above.

Figure 3.1

Distribution of Computing Functions Across All Computing Applications from the 82 Panel Organizations, 1985 and 1993.

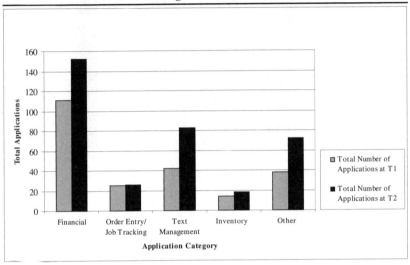

Figure 3.2

Percentage of Panel Organizations Reporting X Number of Applications

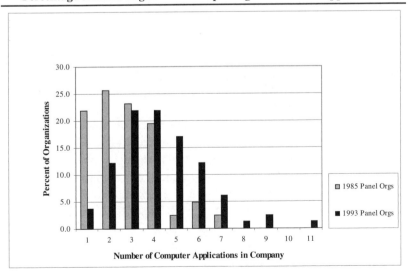

Figure 3.3

Percentage of Panel Organizations Reporting X Number of Checklist Items

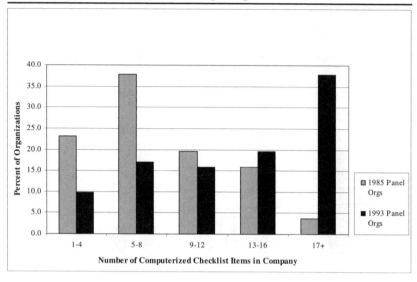

Number of Computerized Checklist Items in Company

* * *

Not all forms of computing growth were captured by our two quantitative measures. Interviews yielded many accounts of what we judged to be significant innovations that simply did not register on these indices. These were cases where specific applications had clearly been enhanced or extended between 1985 and 1993 without registering an increment either on our checklist of computerized activities or our total of qualitatively distinct computer applications. Typically, such "hidden growth" resulted from incremental efforts to extend the capacity of existing computing arrangements by managers or staff who do not necessarily think of themselves as changing something fundamental.

In an attempt to learn a bit about such otherwise uncharted growth, we asked respondents in 1993 if each application reported in 1985 did "anything different from what it was doing at the time of our previous interview." Of those who responded, a majority (115 vs. 85 cases) answered affirmatively. When asked whether the volume of activity (that is, the *amount* of activity, rather than the *kind*) associated with a particular application had changed from 1985 to 1993, the great majority of those responding (100 vs. 39) characterized the application as doing more rather than less over the period of the study.

Sometimes the changes reported in these contexts were minor, but elsewhere they led cumulatively to marked qualitative differences in work relations. Consider the specialized word processing application used by [145] in framing contracts for its forklift sales. The discursive description given (on p. 31 above) was from the interviewer's notes in 1985; at that stage, the application simply entered different elements into standardized contracts being prepared for clients, reducing drudgery for the secretaries in the establishment. By the time of the 1993 interview, management had devised ways to supplement these functions. The system of recording customizing details of contracts now also recorded the ultimate outcome of the sales offer—creating a record of "who sells what and income amounts for each department," according to our interviewer. Thus a system that had originally been a device for streamlining clerical activity now was also a system for monitoring the performance of sales staff.

It appears very common, over the time period covered in these interviews, for applications to have been enhanced along lines like these, so as to "kill two birds with one stone" for those who used them. It was not unusual for such developments to involve increasing monitoring of staff, along with accretion of other standard computing functions. One medium-sized printing company we interviewed in 1985, for example, had recently instated a computer system for monitoring the times its printing equipment was "down," and hence unproductive. One result of having this system, they found, was that their hourly-paid printing staff could no longer deliberately ignore machine breakdowns, so as to generate periods of "paid vacation" for themselves until management discovered that the machines were not working. Computer monitoring of machines had led, apparently unintendedly, to more rigorous control over the work of those who tended them.

Similar examples of incremental qualitative growth abound in these cases. Another comes from our interviews at [163], a company that originally acted simply as a warehouser for various wholesalers, using a computerized inventory system to keep track of where various clients' goods were stored. Increasing the use of one key application, however, made it possible to extend its business. In the words of our interviewer,

[I]n recent years the firm has added billing and receivables to its activities. That is, [163] now takes orders for its clients' goods, ships them out, and then does the billing and receivables for items shipped... These activities were started in an effort to provide a more comprehensive service to [163's] customers...

According to the respondent, these activities have never been performed without the computer system and could not be performed without the computer...

A number of changes have been made in this application in recent years... [These changes have led to] added flexibility in the types of reports that [163] can provide to its clientele, which can now be totally customized according to the clients' needs.

As in countless other areas of social life, the intentions guiding innovation in computing use are no exact guide to the outcomes of the changes that result. Once new computing arrangements are put in place, they set the managerial mind off in directions not necessarily anticipated at the time of the original innovation. As in this case, the existence of computerized routines, and above all that of new data generated by computerization, spur thoughts about new products and services, about cheaper ways of accomplishing long-standing aims and profitable ways of pursuing new ones. We return to this theme in Chapter 6.

In a few cases, the incremental internal evolution of computing applications actually led to *reduction* of the total numbers of applications we documented between 1985 and 1993. This occurred where the activities under one or more application "reached out" symbiotically to fuse with other application. An example is the evolution in computing arrangements reported by [152], a suburban wholesaler of ice cream products with a year-round staff of just nine. The forms of computerization reported in this firm in our first interviews were quite conventional, including one application that did both order entry and inventory control and another devoted to keeping track of accounts receivable; the latter application also generated sales reports.

By the time of our second interview with this organization in 1993, these two applications had become one. In the words of the 1993 interviewer, the new, comprehensive application took over when retailers call in ice cream orders:

Inventory is automatically checked at that time and if items are available, the bill is produced and immediately sent out. If the customer has bad credit with [152], then the staff member who answers the phone will automatically know not to fill the order. The application produces a pick ticket [a slip instructing the delivery person to select the specific item required for delivery to the customer] which is later used for shipping...

In the new application, in other words, orders for goods triggered a chain-reaction of processes ranging from directions to delivery staff to billing of customers—combining activities previously requiring what we defined as two separate applications. In this respect, one would say that the comprehensiveness or sophistication of computing had grown, though the number of distinct computing applications by our definitions had decreased.

Cases like these were not common—when the boundaries between previously distinct computer applications were actually obliterated. But the innovations that occurred in this organization between 1985 and 1993 illustrate what we have come to see as a pervasive phenomenon—the tendency of decision-makers to tinker, often quite imaginatively, with what may begin as relatively simple computing arrangements. The effects of such tinkering on the quantitative measures of computing change that we have been able to employ here may often be tiny or non-existent. But clearly it would be a mistake to miss the changes effected in the over-all role of computing in organizations by these strictly "internal" developments.

Sources and Sequence of Change

Growth in computing capacity—quantifiable and not—was therefore predominant in our panel, though it was highly uneven in form and amount across organizations. Where, then, does it arise? Are additions to computing activities concentrated in one industry or setting, for example, or are they more widely distributed?

Our hypotheses here pointed toward the first of these possibilities. We assumed that organizations heavily involved in accounting activities—banks and other financial institutions, for example—would find it more attractive to add computing than, say, industrial or construction companies. Certainly the literature on computerization acknowledges significant differences in rates of investment in computing across industrial sectors (see for example Landauer 1995, pp. 22-45).

Yet, to our surprise, our panel data show rather little indication of such differences. As the models shown in Appendix 3.2 illustrate, industrial sector predicts very little of the rate of change in levels of computing per staff between 1985 and 1993. Similar conclusions are apparent for other salient independent variables, including region within the metropolitan area; length of time since first computing; and size of organization. The only predictive variables in the model were the two indices of level of computing in 1985. Unsurprisingly, organizations with low levels of computing at the beginning of the panel study were more likely to increase their capacities than those that began the period with greater computing capacity already in place. The picture emerging from these analyses is one of computing as a sort of universal organizational utility, whose acquisition and growth are pursued with equal interest across all sorts of private-sector organizations.

* * *

One of the most widely-intoned themes in commentary on the growth of computing in organizations envisages a fixed succession of stages in the role of computing within any organization—a "natural history," in which standard early manifestations give way predictably to more advanced or mature forms. In the words of James Nolan, one of earliest proponents of such models,

> the planning, organizing and controlling activities associated with managing the computer resource will change in character over a period of time, and will evolve in patterns roughly correlated to four stages of the computer budget: Stage I (computer acquisition), Stage II (intense system development), Stage III (proliferation of controls), and Stage IV (user/service orientation). (1973, p. 399)

Nolan's scheme is conceptually neat, but one has to wonder about the breadth of its empirical application. The notion that computing development within any organization follows a preordained lifecycle sounds eminently plausible. But as far as we can determine, no systematic empirical evidence has been reported showing that such sequences actually occur in any sizeable number of organizations.

Certainly we find little such evidence in this sample. One incongruity between Nolan's model and our findings has to do with the unitary character of organizational computing in his descriptions—as though "computing" was just one form of activity within any establishment. Basic to our findings is the heterogeneity of distinct computing applications within organizations. Thus, what may be true of computing as applied to accounting and financial analysis may have little bearing on uses of the "same" technology for production control or inventory within the same organization. We find little evidence of any pervasive ethos of computing *in general* in these organizations, as distinct from thinking about specific applications.

Our data do make it easy to assess one kind of sequence in the use of computing by organizations: the order of adoption of computing applications with different functions. Appendices 3.3 and 3.4 make this comparison for the basic types of computing discussed above.

These figures make it apparent that our four basic forms of computing are not equally likely to be acquired at different points in computerization. Financial applications are important from the beginning, amounting to nearly forty percent of those first to be adopted, as shown in Table 3.3; as Table 3.4 shows, nearly half again as many financial applications as existed in 1985 were adopted between then and 1993. In comparison, a much greater proportion of all applications devoted to order entry and job tracking are adopted early; only four such applications are reported adopted between the 1985 and 1993 interviews. This finding makes it appear that there exists a finite "need" for computerization of this kind, a need that is fulfilled at an early stage of computerization. Something similar seems to occur with inventory applications; only some 22 percent of these are added between the two points.

Word processing applications, on the other hand, account for a relatively high proportion of all applications added between the two waves of interviews; clearly this need is not readily exhausted in these establishments. We also find it noteworthy that nearly half all the "other" applications are added between 1985 and 1993. This suggests, as we argue further in Chapter 7, that innovation in computing use is apt to be a function of extended acquaintance with more standardized forms of the technology.

Conclusion

The literature on computing abounds with vivid images of sweeping organizational transformation in its wake. The portrait emerging from this analysis is rather different. Instead of being holistic or comprehensive, computing adoption as documented here consists of highly-targeted, *ad hoc* measures. Decision-makers opt for computing, in other words, to solve specific organizational problems. Computing begins with efforts to do familiar things through innovative means; the resulting arrangements appear initially quite continuous with previous practice.

Moreover, the "things" targeted for computerization in most cases appear quite predictable across a heterogeneous variety of organizations. The computing applications we encountered proved to resemble each other far more than we anticipated, with the great majority devoted to four basic organizational functions. These functions—accounting, order entry, text management, and inventory control—are activities that might well be found in virtually any private-sector organization. Except for a durable minority of roughly twenty percent *sui generis* applications, the functions served by computing are very widely shared across organizations that are outwardly quite different.

As expected, for the great majority of establishments in this sample, reliance on computing grew significantly over the period of this study. Such growth appears quite evenly distributed across different types of organizations in our sample. Not only do our quantitative measures show growth in this respect; the details of individual cases also demonstrate various forms of internal evolution, such that computing activities often grow richer and more resourceful, even where they do not register quantitative growth.

Finally, if the uses of computing reported here rarely revamp work roles to the extent envisaged by many authors, they also generally involve fewer conceptual leaps. Few if any of the 691 applications documented at various points in our study seem to have brought sweeping or abrupt transformations of workplace mindsets. Where conceptual changes arise from computerization, we suspect that they occur incrementally, as technology and its users interact at length.

Appendix 3.1

Distribution of Computing Functions Across Eight Industrial Classifications, 1993 Panel Organizations.

	Construction		Discrete Manufact		Process Manufact		Transport/ Communic/ Utilities		Wholesale		Retail		Finance/ Real Estate/ Insurance		Services	
	N	%	N	%	N	%	N	%	N	%	N	%	N	%	N	%
Total Applications	45	100.0	42	100.0	23	100.0	20	100.0	64	100.0	45	100.0	34	100.0	78	100.0
Financial	23	51.1	15	35.7	14	60.9	8	40.0	29	45.3	15	33.3	16	47.1	32	41.0
Order Entry/ Job Tracking	3	6.7	5	11.9	2	8.7	3	15.0	8	12.5	4	8.9	0	0.0	1	1.3
Text Management	11	24.4	9	21.4	3	13.0	3	15.0	16	25.0	11	24.4	10	29.4	20	25.6
Inventory	0	0.0	3	7.1	2	8.7	1	5.0	3	4.7	8	17.8	0	0.0	1	1.3
Other	8	17.8	10	23.8	2	8.7	5	25.0	8	12.5	7	15.6	8	23.5	24	30.8

Appendix 3.2

**Effects of Organization Characteristics on Computing
Growth in Panel Organizations, 1985-1993 (N=82).**

Independent Variables[a]	Percent Change in Applications[b] OR (95% CI)	Percent Change in Checklist Items[c] OR (95% CI)
1985 Low Level of Computing	24.25 (5.17-115.54)***	7.37 (2.21-24.54)**
1985 Total Site Employees	0.38 (0.10-1.41)	1.41 (0.40-4.99)
Number of Months Computing	1.82 (0.44-7.43)	0.69 (0.20-2.43)
Region[d]: Manhattan	0.27 (0.06-1.27)	0.31 (0.07-1.39)
Region: Nassau/Suffolk Cnty	0.99 (0.25-4.00)	1.37 (0.38-5.01)
SIC[e]: Construction/ Transport/Utilities	3.16 (0.43-23.36)	2.99 (0.56-16.00)
SIC: Manufacturing	0.22 (0.04-1.33)	3.04 (0.56-16.43)
SIC: Wholesale/Service	1.20 (0.26-5.54)	0.82 (0.18-3.75)
-2 Log Likelihood	72.42	78.16
Goodness-of-Fit X^2 [Hosmer-Lemeshow]:	8.47, df=8, p=0.389	5.45, df=8, p=0.708
Model Chi-Square	35.28, df=8, p=0.000	25.76, df=8, p=0.001
N	82	82

OR: Odds Ratio, CI: Confidence Interval, +p<.10, *p<.05, **p<.01, ***p<.001

[a] Independent variables dichotomized at medians: 1985 Applications=3; 1985 Checklist=8; 1985 Staff=50; Months Computing=144.

[b] Dependent variable dichotomized at mean: 1=Higher than 79% increase in applications, 0=79% or lower.

[b] Dependent variable dichotomized at mean: 1=Higher than 100% increase in checklist items, 0=100% or lower.

[d] Location of organization (reference group is Brooklyn/Queens)

[e] SIC: Standard Industrial Classification (reference group is retail/financial/insurance)

Note: To predict growth in our two original computing variables we first dichotomized these variables into values above and below their means. Percent change in applications was dichotomized at 79% (predicting companies that increased their applications by more than 79% by 1993) and percent change in checklist items was dichotomized at 100%. We then dichotomized the independent variables at their medians, 1=High, 0=Low. The only exception to this was with the variable 1985 level of computing where 1=Low and 0=High.

Appendix 3.3

Sequence of Application Adoption as of 1993 (N=346)[a].

Application Function

Sequence of Adoption	Total		Financial		Order Entry/ Job Tracking		Text Management		Inventory		Other	
	N	%	N	%	N	%	N	%	N	%	N	%
First	118	34.1	59	39.3	20	76.9	16	19.8	7	38.9	16	22.5
Middle	129	37.3	56	37.3	2	7.7	34	42.0	7	38.9	30	42.3
Last	99	28.6	35	23.3	4	15.4	31	38.3	4	22.2	25	35.2

[a] Five cases unable to determine adoption date.

RE: Table 3.3: Rankings of sequence of application adoption were based on questions in both 1985 and 1993 interviews on the date of adoption of each application. Those reported adopted earliest within any organization were classified "First"; latest were classified "Last." Applications not included in either category were classified as "Middle."

Often more than one application was reported as having been adopted at a single date; we systematically ascribed all such applications to the same classification. If all applications reported within the establishment were reported as adopted at the same time, all were classified "First."

Of a total of 351 applications reported in the panel study cases in 1993, only five could not be ranked because of missing data. (Some eight applications following the above classification scheme, were recorded as *both* "First" and "Last.")

Appendix 3.4

Distribution Across Functional Types of Computing Applications in Place in 1985 and Those Added Between 1985 and 1993 (N=351).

Application Function

	Total		Financial		Order Entry/ Job Tracking		Text Management		Inventory		Other	
	N	%	N	%	N	%	N	%	N	%	N	%
Applications in place as of 1985	223	63.5	106	69.7	22	84.6	42	50.6	14	77.8	39	54.2
Newly adopted applications 1993	128	36.5	46	30.3	4	15.4	41	49.4	4	22.2	33	45.8

4

Monitoring and Control of Work

Among the varied organizations captured in our sample were two computerized restaurants. In these establishments, waiters and waitresses transmitted customers' orders electronically to the kitchen from consoles in the dining room. The system recorded each order and prepared the bill; no other communication between dining room and kitchen staff was permitted.

Such computerized restaurant operations are by no means unusual, it appears, though the establishments apparently do not like to advertise this form of computerization. For reasons that would bear much reflection, the idea of having one's dinner served up by a computer appears much less appealing than, say, the notion of having one's tax returns prepared by computer.

In one of these restaurants, computerization of the dining room had reportedly gone fairly smoothly. The fact that the kitchen could receive orders only through the computer, according to the maitre d' we interviewed, afforded certain significant advantages. For one thing, the electronic communications forestalled the otherwise endemic disputes between servers and kitchen staff over what had been ordered, and when. For another, requiring that all orders be computerized precluded a costly scam, in which customers received expensive items that never appeared on their bills, in exchange for lavish tips. At the same time, the computerized record of all orders promised to enable management to judge whether expensive ingredients were disappearing from the kitchen faster than they were actually being paid for.

Pleased by the apparent success of this effort, the owners of the restaurant decided to extend the same system to the bar. A computer console was installed there, and the bartender was instructed to enter every order in the computerized log before filling it.

Here the rationalizing role of information technology suffered a setback. The bartender, not surprisingly, viewed the change as an imposition of an irksome, superfluous step on his settled routine. It was also a step that was easily ignored, since, unlike the dining room staff, he both accepted and prepared customers' orders. After repeated foot-dragging and complaints, the maitre d' reported, the bartender "accidentally" poured a bottle of Amaretto, that notoriously sticky *digestif*, into the console. At this point, computerization of the bar was suspended.

Most establishments in our study yielded no such colorful anecdotes. But the workplace tensions implicit in this story were evident in many of our interviews. Almost wherever in the workplace it occurs, computing threatens to tap endemic conflicts over knowledge about the work process and control over it. Whatever else computing does, it captures, preserves and transforms information, often recording what might otherwise have gone unnoted, and making it available in settings and to parties where it would not otherwise appear. It is hard to imagine how any technology with these qualities could remain a matter of indifference to the parties concerned.

The Threat of Comprehensive Work Surveillance

Of all the potent images of workplace computing abroad in our culture, perhaps the most influential is that of the-computer-as-relentless-and-unforgiving-monitor-of-job-performance. This vision has the potential to tap everyone's deepest anxieties both about work and technology: it infuses both journalistic and scholarly writing on computing.

In one of the most widely noted studies, Shoshana Zuboff portrayed the effects of sophisticated computerized monitoring systems on the *experience* of work. In one highly automated paper factory, for example, management had developed what they called the Overview System to monitor the continuous processing of wood pulp into paper products. This system

> had been built to read and record key instrument values throughout the plant (more than 2,500 pieces of data) every five seconds. These values could be organized by unit or summarized to provide a bird's eye view of the total operation. The data were available on-line for three days and then were stored indefinitely. This meant that it was not necessary to know in advance what data might be important or why; the data could be retrieved and analyzed at a later date, giving rise to ever new interpretive possibilities. (1988, p. 316)

Zuboff presents a number of accounts of such systems, and makes it clear that all had major impacts on how employees experienced their work. For example, she describes how a telephone company worker begins his day in a highly computerized system:

> He moves toward a computer terminal and enters his password, time, and location. Within seconds, the screen is filled with his assignments for the eight-hour workday. The assigned tasks are listed in the order in which they are to be undertaken, and each task is accompanied by a "price"—the amount of time in which it is to be completed. As he finishes each task, the craftsworker checks in with the computer terminal to note the completed assignment and the amount of time it actually took to do the work. He also checks in to see if his work load for the rest of the day has been altered in any way.... Managers in the central office want to know how workers perform against the prices they are assigned. The system uses these ratios to compute "efficiency ratings" for each worker, ratings that are later used to evaluate performance and that become part of the managerial data base used for determining prices, assigning work loads, and judging organizational efficiency. (p. 318)

Many of us find systems like these inherently menacing. There are two elements to the perceived threat. One is the ability of the systems to know about virtually every element of job performance; the other is the readiness of the organizations involved to act on such knowledge in their treatment of the employees involved. Surely, it may seem, any system capable of such far-reaching scrutiny and action is bound to be invasive of workers' privacy. Zuboff seems to credit such fears in passages like this quotation from a manager in the plant:

> With the Overview System, I can find out everything you did except for what went on in your head. This can be good or bad. It becomes easier to catch people in judgment situations if you have some data to use as a basis. It makes feedback easier and more effective. But if someone makes an obvious mistake, the tendency is to feel that it is easier to fire them than to help train them. (p. 317)

The question is, how widespread are developments like these? To what extent do such overpowering uses of computing represent the emerging standard for workplace monitoring? Here data from our interviews can shed some light.

Both our interviews in 1985 and 1993 included questions on the role of computing in workplace monitoring. In the earlier investigation, interviewers asked whether each application enabled management to "keep closer track of staff." If so, details were sought. In the 1993 telephone interviews, the interviewer asked whether each application involved "any monitoring of staff performance." If the answers were affirmative, the interviewers continued with certain follow-up questions.

Table 4.1.

	1985 Applications (n=541)		1985 Applications from Panel Firms (n=230)		1993 Applications from Panel Firms (n=351)	
Applications Involving Surveillance At Two Time Points, 1985 & 1993.						
	%	N[a]	%	N	%	N[b]
Involves Surveillance	14.0	72	11.7	27	16.1	54
Does Not Involve Surveillance	86.0	444	88.3	203	83.9	281

[a] 25 missing.

[b] 16 missing.

Based on responses to these queries, Table 4.1 shows the proportions of all applications reported to our interviewers that involved some form of surveillance over job performance. The first column in Table 4.1 describes all the 541 applications in the 186 organizations making up our original sample in 1985; the second and third columns describe applications reported in the 82 panel organizations that remained in the study in 1993. Thus the first column includes data on all the organizations described in the second and third columns, in addition to data on those organizations where we were unable to carry out interviews in the second wave of our inquiry.

Table 4.1 makes it clear that use of computing for surveillance over job performance is by no means a rarity. In 1985, slightly more than ten percent of all computing applications reported in our study involved some form of staff performance monitoring. In 1993, the proportion had dropped to a bit more than sixteen percent.

But do the surveillance activities reported here in fact resemble those so vividly described by Zuboff? The wording of our interview questions, after all, was cast in very inclusive terms: Did each particular application serve *at all* for monitoring job performance?

Here are capsule descriptions of five relatively typical surveillance applications from our sample:

Establishment #1, a Manhattan burglar alarm company with 141 staff in 1993. Application 2 runs off the electronic signals continually transmitted from each customer's alarm to the company's central office; among the other signals is an indicator as to whether company inspectors in the field have completed service inspections to determine that the alarms are working properly.

Establishment #7, an outer-borough auto dealership with 85 staff in 1993. Application 2 controls access to the inventory of spare parts. In the words of the interviewer, employees "must enter a personal code each time they use or order a part. Then each part has to be accounted for in the work orders the employees complete."

Establishment #104, an outer-borough veterinary clinic with 29 staff in 1985. Application 1 records time spent and procedures performed by each vet, enabling management to review their work at a glance.

Establishment #166, a suburban manufacturing operation specializing in metal stamping with 37 staff in 1993. Application 2 (1993) analyzes the costs of each job undertaken by the company. These analyses ascribe costs to labor as well as to other factors of production, enabling management to judge the efficiency of specific workers.

Establishment #212, a Manhattan retailer of office furniture with 13 staff in 1993. Application 4 is devoted to sales analysis, enabling management to evaluate profits generated by each sales person and to provide more exact instructions for their sales visits.

We suspect that most readers do not find, in these five cases, quite the threatening qualities of computerized job surveillance intimated by Zuboff. Perhaps the reason is the *comprehensiveness* of the monitoring implied in Zuboff's accounts—that is, the *variety* of different points in any one worker's performance subjected to monitoring. Most cases from our sample, like those described above, involve computerized recording of one or a few relatively discrete work activities. They compare the profitability of various salespersons' sales, for instance, or they note when a single step in a work process by a particular worker is completed. By contrast, what strikes most of us—and worries us—in the cases Zuboff describes is the prospect that the computer might relentlessly, automatically commit to record nearly every action and omission by every worker, all day, every workday. Most readers will probably find this an unacceptable image of work. Yet it is also easy to imagine how management might find it attractive to carry out such thoroughgoing work monitoring.

Do *any* of our surveillance applications approach the pervasiveness of Zuboff's? One of them, perhaps: an application designed to monitor workers' movements within a computerized dairy. We can call this establishment, located in an outer borough of New York City, with 400 staff in 1993, [267]. Management at this factory-like operation had experienced considerable difficulty with what it described as its peripatetic labor force. We chose to carry out a site visit here, after hearing about the application in question during our 1993 telephone interview. In the words of the interviewer who carried out that interview:

In 1992 [this establishment] adopted a computerized time clock application. This machine requires that unionized workers swipe their badges across a plastic plate when they pass through the main doors of the plant. This system then keeps track of not only when the workers are present but also their approximate location at any time during the workday.

[The dairy] is located in several different buildings at this site. As the respondent explained it...it is very easy for workers to get "lost," to sneak out early, to be around but not where they are "supposed" to be. The new system makes it much harder for workers to hide out. It makes it possible for management to tell which particular staff [member] is on duty at any given time, which ones are approaching over-time, which ones had the previous day off, etc.

...the staff has rebelled against this system. When the machines were first installed, they were damaged numerous times. (The respondent says they lost a clock per week when they first got them.) They [the clocks] are now enclosed in steel cases to protect them from vandalism. Also, because workers will swipe each others' cards (to make it look like they are where they are supposed to be or at the plant at all when they are not), the company is trying to install a new system that will read handprints instead of ID cards. The respondent says that the union is trying to block this new system.

The contrast between this and virtually all of our other cases of computerized job surveillance is hard to miss. Here, for one thing, surveillance over job performance was clearly the originating purpose for this system—not simply a second-order consequence of computerization instated for other purposes. Further, management was not merely using the computer to record specific acts that staff were supposed to perform in the course of their jobs. It was instead attempting to record a domain of worker activity that management considered highly *related* to performance of assigned duties. In principle, every movement by every unionized worker from one area of the workplace to another stood to be recorded by this system—on the assumption that those shown to be in the "wrong" place must not be doing what they were paid for.

Few, if any, other job-surveillance applications encountered in our study have these qualities. Virtually all the others seem directed at measuring the activities staff are employed to perform. Consider the computerized communications between serving staff and kitchen in the two restaurants in our sample. The surveillance aspects of these arrangements are easy to recognize. By capturing the timing and content of orders for each waitress and waiter, the system provided management with a condensed account of each day's performance for each staff member. The maitre d' whom we interviewed explained that this made it possible—in principle, though not necessarily in practice—to know which servers had managed to entice diners to order that profit-generating pre-meal drink or special dessert. This system thus recorded more discrete elements of job performance than many of the surveillance applications noted above from our sample. Nevertheless, the restaurant application stopped short of doing what the application in [267] aimed to do: monitoring movement of staff, simply on the assumption that those movements were somehow predictive of their doing what they were hired to do.

The Settings of Computerized Job Surveillance

In one important respect, many surveillance applications from our sample do resemble those described by Zuboff. They work by creating computerized "markers" recording specific acts of job performance. This is the case in Establishment #1 from the list above, for example. The servicing of each burglar alarm registers an (apparently very simple) signal with the central office; that signal in effect shows that one important step in job performance has taken place. The same can be said for any number of other cases—for example the logging of treatments carried out in establishment #104, the veterinary clinic.

Delving through our entire backlog of surveillance applications, we find many that fit this description. These are *job tracking* applications; a large proportion of all computer applications reported in our interviews are of this type. We define such applications as those that create a computerized record of each individual job when the work is first taken on; this record then "follows" the job itself from its first appearance on the agenda of the organization to its completion. At each step of the way, those involved in the work must typically log onto the record, creating in this way an electronic marker of the discharge of their responsibilities. The jobs tracked in this way are as varied as the organizations in our study, ranging from loans in banks to orders of manufactured goods.

Job tracking is one of three broad types of activities that form the context for most computerized work surveillance. The other two are *sales analysis* and *inventory control*. The surveillance aspects of sales analysis (as in establishment #212 above) are obvious. No one in charge of any business is likely to be indifferent to the effectiveness of sales people; computing makes it especially easy to record and analyze such performance. Finally, it should be nearly as apparent why inventory control (as in establishment #7 above) so often has surveillance aspects. Such systems normally record who removes each item of inventory, when, and for what purpose. Such systems serve both to control theft from the organization and to monitor legitimate uses of inventory items.

Analysis of the purposes served by applications involving surveillance shows that the majority are of one of these three types.
Table 4.2 shows this distribution.

Thus, computerized surveillance over job performance is largely
predictable in its forms and settings. It occurs, at least in this representative sample, embedded in processes that clearly have non-computerized equivalents in all sorts of public and private organizations. Note that the non-computerized forms of job tracking, sales
analysis, and inventory control are apt to involve job supervision in
their own right; one should not assume, in other words, that com-

Table 4.2

**Functions of Applications Involving Surveillance at
Two Time Points, 1985 & 1993.**

	1985 Applications (n=541)		1985 Applications from Panel Firms (n=230)		1993 Applications from Panel Firms (n=351)	
	%	N	%	N	%	N
Total Surveillance Applications	100.0	72	100.0	27	100.0	54
Financial						
Financial/Accting: General	5.6	4	7.4	2	7.4	4
General Ledger	2.8	2	0.0	0	5.6	3
Accounts Receivable	11.1	8	3.7	1	5.6	3
Accts Payable	2.8	2	3.7	1	1.9	1
Billing, Invoice	5.6	4	7.4	2	3.7	2
Job Costing	5.6	4	7.4	2	7.4	4
Sales Analysis	16.7	12	18.5	5	9.3	5
Other Financial	1.4	1	3.7	1	7.4	4
Order Entry/Job Tracking						
Order Entry/Job Tracking: General	4.2	3	0.0	0	0.0	0
Order Entry Only	11.1	8	7.4	2	5.6	3
Fuller Job Tracking	4.2	3	3.7	1	5.6	3
Text Management						
Text Management: General	2.8	2	0.0	0	1.9	1
Standard WP	0.0	0	0.0	0	0.0	0
Other Text Mgmt	1.4	1	0.0	0	0.0	0
Inventory						
Inventory: General	0.0	0	0.0	0	1.9	1
Raw Materials	2.8	2	3.7	1	3.7	2
Replacement Parts	5.6	4	11.1	3	9.3	5
Finished Goods	1.4	1	3.7	1	3.7	2
Other						
Other	15.3	11	18.5	5	20.4	11

puting somehow brings about monitoring of work performance in these settings where there was none before.

Note also something distinctive about computerized job surveillance in such settings. In these cases, monitoring people is concomitant of the monitoring of *things*—work orders, sales, or inventories. The restaurant whose story is recounted at the beginning of this chapter, for instance, did not computerize *only* to generate new information on work performance. Another management objective was to rationalize communications by obviating miscues between dining room and kitchen. Similarly, the many inventory control applications like the one in establishment #7 above were as much systems for keeping track of things as of people. The only case in our sample where computerized surveillance appears to be exclusively created for monitoring people, as distinct from monitoring objects or work processes, was the application described above from [267].

Directions of Change

We have stated that we do not discern, in the cases of computerized job surveillance reported in our sample, quite the threatening situation conveyed in Zuboff's accounts. But some might suspect that her cases simply represent the shape of things to come. The qualitative developments in job surveillance noted in our rather ordinary organizations, it might be argued, are simply the embryo that will eventually develop into the full-blown, all-encompassing forms described by her. In this view, given the ingenuity of management and the inherent possibilities of technology, what appear as circumscribed and discrete forms of monitoring today are bound to grow into all-embracing processes.

It would be rash to dismiss this possibility. Certainly our study provides some examples of the evolution of computerized workplace surveillance from less to more sophisticated forms. Consider our establishment #247, a Manhattan clothing retailer we will call Downtown Shops. One of its computer applications is a job-tracking and inventory-control program. This registers the establishment's acquisition of merchandise and follows the goods through the organization from then until the moment where the point-of-sale cash machine records the sale. As in many establishments, the computerized count of items in stock is adjusted for each purchase registered by the point-of-sale (POS) system on the shop floor. And again, as in many other inventory control systems, this application is used to signal "shrinkage"—that is, pilferage—though this particular application cannot typically identify those responsible for shrinkage. In this respect, the surveillance applications of computing did not seem to change much within this establishment in the years immediately before our first interview in 1985.

But a more subtle evolution in computerized job surveillance had occurred in the role played by this application in the work of the *buyers*—those who select the merchandise that will appear as the store's stock-in-trade. As in any retail establishment, buyers in Downtown Shops succeed by choosing lines of merchandise that will in be turn chosen by customers. Thus they have an intense personal interest in current sales of "their" items, and top management has a parallel interest in monitoring the profitability of various buyers' choices.

In the years leading up to our first interview in 1985, Downtown Shops developed some striking innovations in these respects. The application that originally calculated the profitability of buyers' choices well after the fact was modified to create a running evaluation of these choices and to reward or penalize the buyers in "real time." To capture the full subtlety of this application, we quote in detail from the 1985 interviewer's acute account:

> [The Vice President for Merchandise Control]...along with Head Merchandising Manager (who is President of the firm) put together a plan for each season... They are setting the boundaries, so to speak, for the buyers.
> The plan takes into account several factors: inventory stock (leftover stock); price change plans (items that are to be discounted) and sales planning for the next season.
> The President generally sets an overall goal for the firm, say, to do 5% more in sales next year overall. Then they work down, department by department, looking at last year's sales data and deciding, say, that men's shirts should sell 5% more, men's belts has sold 3% more every year for 5 years, so they should sell 3% more...[etc.]

The sales planning described here is undoubtedly paralleled in countless businesses, computerized and not. But some additional features of the application involve a subtlety of monitoring of buyers' choices that would probably be impossible without the computer:

> The [resulting] plan then gives the buyers a total dollar amount...to use the next season. This, however, is constantly adjusted by the computer...[using] POS data. If buyer A is doing very well and his stock is moving fast, he will automatically be allocated more buying money according to the plan. If buyer B is doing lousy in his department, his amount will be scaled back. The way this works is that each buyer gets an "open to buy report" which gives the dollar amount he is allowed to use that

week. This is based on the total goal set forth in the master plan and how much he has spent and how much he has sold (from POS data). So, if buyer A is buying a lot but also selling a lot, his "open to buy money" will continue to be a lot. If buyer B has bought a lot but sold very little, his "open to buy" money will quickly shrink to zero.

Besides staying within these dollar parameters, the buyer has discretion to use the money as he wishes. He uses sales data...to decide how to spend the money. However, there is a catch: the buy requisitions make two stops: one at [the Vice-President's] desk and one at the President's. [The Vice-President] is looking at the dollar figure for each purchase made by a buyer and making sure it stays within guidelines and that the buyer isn't using his money too fast. He is also looking at broad inventory levels to make sure the buyer isn't taking on too much stock...

The buyers, then, are certainly under more scrutiny. Before the computer and POS, the President and [Vice-President] only had data to the department and classification level...and often this was incorrect...

As the interviewer notes in conclusion, these buyers are clearly subject to much closer and more discriminating scrutiny under this computerized system than under its less sophisticated predecessor.

This computerized monitoring of buyers' job performance strikes us as both subtle and powerful. Yet the surveillance involved is of quite a different kind from that described by Zuboff—or the system in use at [267], the closely-monitored dairy described above. It is not that the buyers are monitored at a great many points in their daily performance. Instead, certain quite discrete but crucial data about their performances—i.e. the profitability of items that they purchase—are subject to immediate and highly analytical monitoring, resulting in very quick positive or negative feedback from management. The ability conferred by the computer to "reach more deeply" into these processes within the organization enables management to control buyers' activities more closely. Therefore we have a classic case in which information that was always somehow "there" within the establishment becomes, via the computer, available so as to transform relationships between management and staff.

What conclusions are we to draw from such cases regarding the future of computerized work? Perhaps some analysts would see in a case like this support for an idea that might be drawn from Zuboff's accounts—that simpler forms of computerized job monitoring are bound to grow more comprehensive over time. In the sharpest version of this view, all forms of computerized workplace surveillance are as though on a conveyor belt. Those that have not yet reached the intensity described in Zuboff's case studies have only to await the virtually inevitable realization of their surveillance potentials.

But we think that such a "conveyor belt" interpretation goes well beyond any available evidence. It assumes, for example, that employers are invariably *interested* in collecting as many data as possible about their employees' on-the-job-activities. We see no *a priori* reason to embrace this assumption.

Consider the many inventory control applications uncovered in our study—systems that note items added to and removed from various inventories, and which also often record the identity of the staff involved. Management interest in monitoring such information is obvious and likely to remain a feature of organizational life for the foreseeable future. But will the extent of information sought by management as a means of monitoring inventory necessarily continue to grow? Or will the relatively discrete data collected under the inventory control systems noted in our interviews suffice? We feel that any categorical answer to such a question is premature.

Values at Stake in Workplace Monitoring

Ultimately, efforts to assess the dangers posed by computerized workplace surveillance force us to confront issues that cannot be resolved solely through empirical assessment. At stake are questions of ultimate value—to wit, how we conceive the essential goods and bads in the monitoring of workplace performance, by computing or any other means. It turns out that these questions are by no means simple.

Nearly any commentator is apt to affirm the desirability in principle of respecting workers' privacy on the job, and of carrying out job supervision with justice and discretion. The question is, how are we to evaluate the impact of surveillance practices like those considered above on such *desiderata*? Is *all* computerized job surveillance to be regarded as *ipso facto* evil? Some commentators seem to take this position. Barbara Garson, in her highly readable *The Electronic Sweatshop*, advocates an outright ban on computerized job surveillance, at least when applied to individual job performance (1988, p. 224). Her conviction is that the new information technologies are inherently more insidious than conventional job monitoring:

> Before electronic supervision, human supervisors were stationed throughout factories and offices in such a way that they duplicated the entire production process in outline. This shadow or silhouette work force was costly and cumbersome. To achieve complete supervision the company would have had to hire a full-time foreman for every worker.

But electronic monitoring doesn't interfere with workflow. Statistics are collected unobtrusively, seemingly as a byproduct of work. (1988, p. 223)

Contra Garson, we can see no grounds to conclude that computerized job monitoring is *categorically* more destructive to crucial values in the experience of work than conventional techniques. It is hard to imagine any viable workplace in which worker output is not subject to some form of management scrutiny. And if evaluation of staff performance is essential to any organization, we see no reason why monitoring by a computer might not, in principle, be fairer, more balanced, or more discreet than old-fashioned direct supervision by managers.

A few accounts from our study support this point. During the early pilot interviews, our team met with a young front-line manager in a company manufacturing medical equipment. One of the computer applications she used was a job tracking system. This worked essentially as did the job tracking programs described above: not only did it track orders through their gestation within the organization, it also recorded key performances by the staff involved in each order. But far from resenting the computerized monitoring, this informant expressed approval for it:

Every step in the processing of each order required that the responsible parties "log on" and "log off" indicating that they had fulfilled their responsibilities. Asked if she found the electronic reporting requirement irksome, the informant said she did not. She insisted that having a computerized record of exactly what she had and had not done forestalled her being held responsible when things went wrong that were none of her doing. She preferred the computerized monitoring system to the conventional supervision practices that it replaced.

We hardly draw any categorical conclusions from stories like these—any more than from the disturbing accounts recorded by Zuboff or Garson. As in so many other contexts, the potential roles that might be played by computers in these situations strike us as almost endlessly varied. We have no difficulty in imagining the imposition of computerized job surveillance in such a way as to make work less private and more demeaning. But we think it would be premature to categorize such effects as the only possible outcomes of computerization.

* * *

Whatever one's assessment of the forms taken by computerized job surveillance, certain questions of ultimate value remain. If a measure of accountability for workers' job performance is assumed, and total scrutiny of every moment of every working day is held offensive, where is one to draw the line?

One possible rule of thumb might be based on a distinction between monitoring performances that actually represent the essential "output" of a job *versus* attention to other characteristics or behaviors of staff. Management scrutiny—computerized or not—over the first category might be held acceptable, but not over the second. Under this rule, management could freely note the number of meals served by waitresses, or the profitability of loans made by bank vice-presidents, or the speed with which plumbers carried out service calls. But it would be unacceptable to collect or scrutinize information on time spent by employees in the workplace rest rooms, or workers' attitudes toward unionization, or their cholesterol levels. These forms of surveillance would be disallowed on the grounds that they target matters at most indirectly related to employees' achievement of the results for which they were hired.

Such a standard would call into question systems like the one discussed above in [267]. The movements of workers from one part of the plant to another, one might argue, are only inferentially related to their performance of their jobs. But note that this same principle would give no grounds for limiting surveillance practices like the close monitoring of buyers' choices developed by Downtown Shops [247]. For there the computerized surveillance, though unquestionably intense, was just as unquestionably relevant to evaluating the effectiveness of the buyers' work.

In that case, the sophisticated computer monitoring system described to our interviewer clearly has resulted in closer—and presumably more anxiety-provoking—monitoring for the buyers subjected to it. But again, not all potentials for such ratcheting up of surveillance via the computer are necessarily realized. Many writers, including Garson (1988, p. 10) and Flaherty (1989, p. 3), have speculated about the oppressive prospect of subjecting typists to surveillance of every single keystroke throughout the working day. The example is certainly disturbing. Most of us would agree that such usage would indeed amount to degradation of privacy and autonomy on the job, yet it is easy to see how it might represent an effective tool of management interests. But in light of the widespread comment on such possibilities, we were struck to discover that our sample turned up no monitoring of this type. Out of a total of fifty-four computing applications entailing some aspect of workplace surveillance in 1993, none involved the monitoring of keyboarding. This despite the fact that some eighty-three (or 23.7%) of all the applications reported in our 1993 interviews were word processing applications.

Other Work Quality Issues

Workplace monitoring is obviously but one of many ways in which computing impinges on the quality of work life. Computerization also alters the content of work, the social interactions of working groups, and the most elementary social structures of the workplace. Here, as virtually everywhere else in commentary on computing, the expectations range from the baleful to the fulsome.

Pessimists are convinced *a priori* that computing will be the avenue by which all meaningful content and worker autonomy will ultimately be wrung out of the labor process. The classic statement of this position is Harry Braverman's *Labor and Monopoly Capital* (1974). Commenting specifically on the effects of computing on clerical work, he wrote:

> As work has been simplified, routinized, and measured, the drive for speed has come to the fore.... And with the economies furnished by the computer system and the forcing of the intensity of labor come layoffs which selectively increase the tendency to factory-like work. (p. 335)

A few pages later, he added:

> So far as the traditional grades of office labor are concerned, the computerization of office accounting procedures further weakens the position of those skilled in the system as a whole, particularly bookkeepers... The decline was continued, especially in banking, by the development of electronic bookkeeping machines, which complete the conversion of bookkeepers into machine operators and at the same time reduce the demand for them sharply... (pp. 338-40)

Needless to say, computing enthusiasts have declaimed just as categorically to the opposite effect. For example, management consultant Paul Strassman adopts a familiar missionary tone in his remarks:

> My premise is that computers are the single most important technological means for assuring the future growth of society's productivity. They are therefore the single most important source of increased personal wealth as well as the basis for improvement of the quality of life in the workplace. (1985, p. xvii)

Our own study provides less detailed information on the quality of work experience than it does on a number of other points. The interviews we carried out with management informants did not always afford the opportunity to examine computer-induced job changes from the standpoint of ordinary workers. Only where management was especially forthcoming did we actually have the chance to observe at any length the conduct of computerized work, or to discuss it with workers. But where we did, the interviews often yielded some striking views of their experiences.

Some of these were nothing if not consistent with Braverman's pessimistic vision of work robbed of skill and discretion. Consider our interviewer's account of the work of clerks in our establishment 115, a highly computerized fast food establishment:

> The cashier pushes buttons on the register corresponding to the items and quantities ordered and NOT to the prices. The register has the prices in memory, calculates tax, provides the total and calculates the change. It also prints out a receipt which the cashier uses to select the items for the order (in other words, they can look at the receipt while selecting the order)...

Recounting the manager's views on the effects of this system on staff, the interviewer continues,

> [The manager] feels that the pace has increased compared to any mechanical system and it has reduced skill requirements. People don't have to be able to calculate change, the machine tells them the change. They also don't have to remember any prices (in fact, I was told that the cashiers don't even know the prices without tax, they only know them with tax, because that is what the register shows).... On mechanical registers, they could enter the wrong price, here if they hit a button for the item, they have to charge the correct price.

Note that, besides their effect on the content of work, these computerized routines do involve surveillance over staff performance. As the interviewer points out, "the only way to cheat...is to give away the food without entering it on the register at all"; if this were done to any extent, he points out, the computerized inventory control system would soon call attention to the missing ingredients.

But not all the stories turned up in our interviews follow this pattern. Consider this account from a pilot interview done in 1984, as we were still developing the final form for the first-wave interviews that began the following year. This interview took place in a small, outer-borough business that had recently computerized its accounting operation. The owner directed us to the establishment's long-time bookkeeper, a quiet lady in her early sixties.

The respondent reported that she had been terrified on learning that her work was to be computerized. She knew nothing of computers and was convinced that it was too late in life for her to learn. She nearly opted for early retirement, she reported, rather than attempting to learn the new technology. But by the time of our interview, she had become a computer enthusiast. She insisted that the accounting software purchased for her use took care of what she had always regarded as the most boring aspects of her work—writing checks, for example, or tallying long columns of figures. What was left were the parts that she had always enjoyed, and continued to enjoy under the new technology.

Nothing in our investigation would warrant the conclusion that stories of this kind are more representative than the one that preceded it. From the fragmentary information on job content available in the interviews, it would appear that most computerization stories are far more mixed or ambiguous than either of these two on this count. But the very diversity of these accounts does leave us skeptical of any categorical "computing effects" on job quality.

A number of researchers have reached similar conclusions. One of the best empirical studies of computerization in the workplace illustrates precisely this point. This is an article by Robert Kraut, Susan Dumais and Susan Koch reporting their before-and-after study of the customer service offices of "a large public utility," which sounds very much like a telephone company (1989, p. 221). Using questionnaires, the authors carefully measured the attitudes of some 169 respondents in several offices responsible for communications with customers over billing, service inquiries, and related matters. These workers spent much of their time consulting customers' account records and negotiating with the customers by phone. The change that occurred between the two waves of data-intake was the computerization of customer records, replacing a microfiche system that had been in use for years. This development was accompanied by certain physical changes in the workspace, in such matters as the extent to which workers could see one another at work. Management sought by these changes to increase workers' ease in access to certain key records, and to reduce their discretion over certain aspects of their work.

On the main productivity variables, Kraut and his associates did find improvement in the before-and-after comparison. By contrast, most variables reflecting employee satisfaction, in most of the work settings, showed a decline. To summarize a rich and nuanced study, it appeared that management had indeed succeeded in making key forms of work easier and more efficient, at the cost of removing much of its interest for most respondents. Respondents reported more negative attitudes toward computerized work over the course of the study, even as they described themselves growing more confident in their use of the machines.

But these "computing effects" were in fact highly contextual. Kraut et al. found that the computerization program had produced the strongest negative reactions among staff in offices dealing with residential customers. Offices dealing with business customers— generally less regimented to start with—showed less marked negative effects of computing on work attitudes (1989, p. 233).

Moreover, the study as a whole makes it clear that conceiving computerization as a force with a fixed "impact" in organizational life—like the force of a projectile striking an inert object—is inappropriate. The "computerization" of the office described could have been accomplished in countless ways, the form taken in the study being only one. And the "effects" of any of these alternate computerization programs would almost certainly vary, according to various pre-existing characteristics of the settings.

Accordingly, we remain skeptical of the search for unique and robust computing "effects" in settings like these. If our own results settle anything, it is that the new information technologies can and indeed do play a wide variety of roles in shaping the experience of work. But we find no reason to see that the positive or negative "effects" of computerization are dictated by the technology itself. Whether the computerized workplaces of a generation from now turn out to be more or less humane than those of the present, we believe, will be shaped more by the sensitivity of human innovators than by characteristics of the technologies, strictly speaking. Some readers may find this conclusion somehow less dramatic than they might wish. But it does at least imply wide latitude for enlightened efforts to make the best of what are obviously far-reaching changes in work.

5

Employment and Efficiency*

Disagreements on other matters notwithstanding, there is one point about computerization that most commentators find almost self-evident: computing is transforming our lives, it is agreed, through a tour de force of superior efficiency. As so many have insisted, computing is simply *a better* way—a better route, it would seem, to almost any destination. Just as motorized transport has relentlessly superseded the horse, or as surgery has displaced folk remedies for appendicitis, computing is bound to crowd out its retrograde competitors. Thus, word processing has all but obliterated typewriting; e-mail is bound to prevail over letter writing; computerized reservation systems will displace manual booking; computerized production controls will outstrip craft labor; and, for all we know, computerized teaching will leave face-to-face instruction by university faculty an anachronism.

One constantly notes assertions to these effects couched in terms of specific activities. Only somewhat more rarely does one encounter the generic version—the contention that information and the technologies for using it represent a kind of generalized resource, fuel for machinery that plays the same role in the information age that petroleum did for the age of manufacturing. Often these statements convey an unmistakable missionary zeal, especially when couched in terms of organizational change:

> Information has been referred to as 'the fourth resource' after money, people and property/equipment...it is vital to manage the increasingly important resource of information...as some of the concepts of IM [information management] become widespread, we will see the nature of work change dramatically...

* The authors thank Monique Centrone for much useful advice on the statistical analyses reported in this chapter.

Information is the key element in virtual organizations because it is the intellect, knowledge and skills of its members which are the organization's most valuable asset. This means that information and its use will become paramount and hence information will be recognized as the first *resource*. Consequently, its management should not be left to chance and solutions developed in an *ad hoc* way... It is essential to choose the right tool for the job. (Parsons 1996, pp. 60-61)

These words were written by an enthusiast of computing in management. But such hortatory statements also draw support from more strictly sociological accounts of the generic role of computing in fostering efficiency. Perhaps the most noted exponent of this vision is Daniel Bell, the sociologist whose writings on the future of computing have been as influential as any:

What is distinctive about the new intellectual technology is its effort to define rational action and to identify the means of achieving it...the desirable action is a strategy that leads to the optimal or 'best' solution; i.e., one which either maximizes the outcome or...tries to minimize the losses. (1973, pp. 30-31)

The striking thing is that convictions of this kind are equally potent in the thoughts of computer admirers and of those who fear the social repercussions of the new technologies. Optimists like Shoshona Zuboff, for example, and pessimists like Henry Braverman share the conviction that the quest for efficiency underlies the pervasive spread of computing in human affairs. For Braverman, of course, this quest for efficiency comes at the cost of removing both discretion and skill from work. For Zuboff, by contrast, computerization may, at best, improve both the returns on capital and the rewards of work to workers.

Even technological optimists, however, are apt to acknowledge that the benefits to be derived from computing will not come without a price. At least in the short run, as Zuboff and countless others emphasize, members of computerizing organizations will have to adapt to jarring changes in the routines of, and very assumptions underlying, their work.

And some workers, most analysts agree, will have to find other work altogether. One of the results most frequently ascribed to computerization is the elimination of jobs, as the new technologies are adopted as substitutes for human labor. Leontieff and Duchin did no more than express standard economic wisdom when they wrote:

[T]he intensive use of automation [including computing] will make it possible to achieve over the next 20 years significant economies in labor relative to the production of the same bills of goods with the mix of technologies in use. Over 11 million fewer workers are required in 1990, and over 20 million fewer in 2000 [under scenarios modeled by the authors for continued adoption of new technologies]. (1986 p. 12)

Obviously, the two elements of this perception go hand in hand: computing is generically more efficient than other ways of doing things; and as those efficiencies are recognized, they will manifest themselves in displacement of human labor.

All this makes good theoretical sense—which would suffice, if not for discordant empirical findings. Many researchers have found great difficulty in demonstrating the productivity gains presumed to result from computerization. In a famous epigram, MIT economist Robert Solow noted that "You can see computing everywhere but in the productivity statistics" (1987, p. 36).

If computing works as most people intuitively expect, gains in productivity should be readily manifest. Investment in computing ought to bring higher returns to any company than allocation of equivalent resources for human labor or other uses. But considerable research on the topic over the years since Solow's remarks has produced highly contradictory evidence on the subject.

True, some empirical studies have shown the sorts of positive effects originally expected on productivity. Lichtenberg (1993), for example, assembled data on expenditures for computing equipment and information system staff in more than 220 large companies between 1988 and 1991. He concluded that there were "substantial 'excess returns' to investment in computer capital" (p. 25); he reaches similar conclusions on computer-related labor. Similar findings are reported by Brynolfsson and Hitt (1993) and Dewan and Min (1997) in their analyses of a data-set on computing and other investments in 380 large firms between 1987 and 1991. In more recent writings, a number of these same authors (e.g. Dewan and Kraemer 1998; Brynjolfsson and Hitt 1998) have continued to press their case, while acknowledging some apparent contradictions in published evidence on the subject.

By contrast, a number of other studies seem to sustain the paradox that Solow alluded to (see Attewell 1994 for an authoritative review of these studies). One author concluded, after reviewing a variety of correlational studies of the relation between computing investment and productivity, that "there is no conclusive evidence as to the profitability of [computing as an] investment..." (Franke 1987, p. 151). Another author more recently commented "...most business investments in computers have yielded significantly lower returns than investments in bonds at market interest rates" (Landauer 1995, p. 13). A third has described the alleged payoffs of computerization as "the big lie of the information age" (Shrage 1997, p. 178).

On the issue of tradeoffs between employment and computerization, results of empirical inquiry have been particularly ambiguous. *Contra* the expectations articulated by Leontieff and Duchin, a number of researchers have actually found *positive* associations between investment in computing and growth in employment. As one pair of authors commented, after analyzing the same data set used by Brynjolfsson and others cited above, computing "...rather than being aggregate labor-saving, increases in [IT] tend to be labor-using" (Morrison and Berndt 1991, p. 1).

Debate on these issues continues at the time of this writing. Some recent authors have pointed to the fact that productivity growth in the United States, after decades of relative decline, began to rise again in the 1990s—suggesting that computing is responsible for the surge. But this broad historical association hardly establishes causality. What needs to be demonstrated is really quite exacting—to wit, that investment in computing, at the level of the enterprise, is both associated with productivity growth and prior to such growth. One must consider the possibility that causality between company profitability and acquisition of computing actually works in the opposite direction to what we intuitively assume. It could plausibly be, for example, that the diffuse cultural associations of computing make it attractive for companies with rich cash flows to flaunt their use of it—e.g. as a symbol of success or of progressive status.

Computing, in other words, might simply be a *marker* for profitability, rather than a cause of it. There can be little doubt that such relationships can readily occur—as demonstrated in a recent study of the correlates of workers' use of various tools on the job. Using a combination of data on jobs in America and Germany, DiNardo and Pischke (1997) demonstrate that computer use is strongly associated with higher wages—an observation taken by some analysts as evidence that the technology imparts high productivity. But the authors show that similar wage advantages attach to "on-the-job use of calculators, telephones, pens or pencils, or for those who work sitting down" (p. 291). The point is obvious: no one would claim that the addition of pens or pencils *caused* productivity gains in these instances; accordingly, one must be guarded about drawing similar conclusions on the role of computing.

Research Strategy and Variables

Our study can shed meaningful light on some of these debates because of its panel design. Instead of struggling to interpret associations between computing use and revenues or staffing within organizations at a single point in time, we can analyze differences across organizations associated with their addition of more and less computing between 1985 and 1993.

Unlike most economists' studies of these matters, ours did not seek to record dollar figures for investment in computing. We were skeptical about the reliability of data that might be provided by establishments in our sample on these points, given that the investments in question often took place over many years prior to our interviews. But we did have the two measures of extent of computing discussed in previous chapters: the number of qualitatively distinct computer applications, and the total of activities reported to be computerized from our standardized checklist of possibilities. These measurements provide indices both for the extent of computerization within establishments at the beginning of the study, and for changes in these levels between the two data intakes.

As it turns out, we have a skeptical report on the "effects" of computerization in the eighty-two organizations making up our panel. Contrary to expectations, we ultimately conclude that computerization showed a net tendency to *increase* staffing in these organizations over the period of the study. And we have been unable to show that computerization makes a significant net difference in the proxy variables used to measure change in efficiency in these establishments.

In the analyses to follow, we trace the relations between computerization and a number of other variables, including:

- Industrial Sector

- Region within Metropolitan New York

- Staff size of establishment, and change in it over time

- A composite index of computerization, and change in it over time

- Company revenues, and change in these over time

- Efficiency (two indices, explained below)

To measure computerization, we relied on a composite index based on the two computing variables used in the analyses shown in Appendix 3.2. This measure gives equal weight to our two key indices, the number of distinct computer applications reported in each establishment, and the number of checklist activities reported to be computerized. A table showing intercorrelations of these and other variables used in the following analyses, and further details on the construction of the computing variable, appear in Appendix 5.1.

* * *

Effects on Employment. If views like those of Leontieff and Duchin hold true, we should expect computing to substitute for human labor. Effects of this kind should be readily demonstrable, given the considerable variability in rate at which establishments added computing over the period under study. One would expect organizations from our sample that computerized more to be less likely to add (or more likely to reduce) staff than those that computerized less—controlling for all other changes over time.

Such thinking came as naturally to our management informants as it does to most economists. In 1985, for example, all respondents were asked how many extra employees would be needed, if not for computer use at the firm. Fifty-eight percent of respondents in those interviews claimed that staffing needs would increase by at least one employee without computing. Similarly, a question in the 1993 interview asked respondents to judge the effects of specific computer *applications* on employment levels: had each application caused a rise in staffing requirements, a decline, or neither? Some thirteen percent of applications were described as resulting in reduced staffing, as against six percent reported to result in staffing gains.

To our surprise, however, our analyses revealed that rates of computerization among our panel organizations between 1985 and 1993 were *positively* associated with staffing changes. As Appendix 5.2 shows, predicted odds of *increasing* staff between the two points were 8.57 times greater for organizations with a high increase in computing than for those with lower rates of computerization. Computerization, this analysis shows, proved to be an even stronger predictor of growth in total staff than increase in sales between the two points. Clearly these organizations, in aggregate, show none of the employment-dampening effects so widely expected to result from the new technology.

Effects on Efficiency. In addition to its expected effects on employment—and concomitant with such effects—computing is widely expected to enhance the efficiency of organizations. Efficiency is a multifarious concept; obviously, no one statistic could possibly capture all the implications of this term. But one direct manifestation of efficiency, we judged, was the ability of the economic unit to avoid bankruptcy in a competitive environment. Accordingly, we checked which of the companies originally sampled in 1985 had declared bankruptcy. County court records showed that some sixteen of the original 186 firms had done so by 1993. We examined the effects of our two computing variables as of 1985 on bankruptcy, regressing bankruptcy status in 1993 (coded as a dummy variable) on firm age in 1985, 1985 sales, staffing, and computing variables. Neither computing measure had a statistically significant effect on bankruptcy.

Another measure of efficiency that we sought to exploit was company earnings per share of stock—a statistic often used as an index of productivity. This is information that publicly traded firms are legally required to provide to the Security and Exchange Commission, and which the SEC in turn makes available to researchers. Since most companies in our sample are not publicly traded, however, we could not use the SEC statistics in every case. But we did determine that, in the twenty cases where SEC figures were available, percentage change in sales per site employee between 1985 and 1993 was positively correlated (.86) with percentage change in earnings per share. Therefore, as one widely-accepted measure of a firm's efficiency increases or decreases (as a function of original levels of the same), so does our measure of firm efficiency. Accordingly, we have used changes in sales per staff as a proxy for changes in efficiency over the period of our study.

In a series of analyses parallel to those of change in staffing levels between 1985 and 1993, shown in Appendix 5.3, we sought to identify the determinants of change in this efficiency variable. These results do nothing to dissipate the productivity paradox. Unsurprisingly, the overwhelming determinant in percent change in sales per staff between 1985 and 1993—our index of change in efficiency—was percent change in over-all sales. Net of this influence, change in our composite computing variable between 1985 and 1993 proved virtually without influence on this dependent variable.

In Quest of Cost-Effectiveness

Surely these findings offer food for thought for anyone concerned to explain the growth of computing and similar technologies. Both managers interviewed in our study and mainstream economic thinking led us to expect computerization to be associated with reduced staffing and enhanced efficiency. But aggregate results from our panel failed to uphold either expectation. Could it be that those closest to the decision to computerize in fact had an imperfect grasp of the economic consequences of their decisions?

In fact, some alternative theoretical views of technological change render these ambiguous findings less puzzling. Earliest among these is that of Jacques Ellul, the French commentator who conceives technological change more as a source of needs than as a solution to them. In Ellul's view, the reader will recall, the growth of technological systems stems from a particular mindset whose distinctive feature is the assumption that all human "problems" admit of technological solutions. Failure of technological measures to produce results expected of them thus does not lead to condemnation of the technology. Instead, planners simply seek to apply technological means more vigorously—for example, by invoking new technological measures to realize the unattained effects of other technologies, or to counteract their undesirable "side effects." In this view, the growth of technological systems is more like drug addiction—where every usage generates the "need" for more—than, say, like taking prescription drugs to solve medical problems. From such a viewpoint, no one should be surprised that the aggregate, measurable results of computerization do not always resemble the visions of decision-makers.

Rob Kling is the present-day analyst of computing who has taken a view closest to Ellul's. In an important article, Kling and Iacono view the diffusion of computing as the manifestation of what they call a "social movement." In their words,

> During the last 20 years, CMs [computerization movements] have helped set the stage on which the computer industry expanded. As this industry expands, vendor organizations...also become powerful participants in persuading people to automate... But vendor actions alone cannot account for the widespread mobilizations of computing in the United States. They feed and participate in it; they have not driven it. Part of the drive is economic, and part is ideological. The ideological flames have been fanned as much by CM advocates as by marketing specialists from the computing industry. Popular writers like Alvin Toffler and John Naisbett and academics like Daniel Bell

have stimulated enthusiasm for the general computerization movement and provided organizing rationales (e.g., transition to a new "information society") for unbounded computerization. Much of the enthusiasm to computerize is a by-product of this writing and other ideological themes advanced by CMs. (1988, p. 240)

"Collective behavior" may be a more exact sociological term for what Kling and Iacono have in mind here than "social movement." The force that they identify as driving the extension of computing is a diffuse, socially-propagated and self-sustaining enthusiasm—embodying unshakable assumptions of the beneficial tendencies of the technology, and resisting any critical confrontation with evidence.

Among contemporary students of organizations, these skeptical approaches have their parallel in what has come to be called "the New Institutionalism" (Powell and DiMaggio 1991). Proponents of this rather diffuse set of doctrines cast their position as an alternative to strictly economic models of organizational change. Many important innovations in organizations, they insist, cannot reasonably be accounted for by anything so simple as cost-benefit calculation. For one thing, costs and benefits are simply not sufficiently clear-cut; the nature of choices to be made, and the identities of those who choose, are open questions. To simplify a bit, one might say that, for the New Institutionalists, the key question is *what kinds of costs* are considered, and who pays them.

In this view, organizations are self-justifying and mutually mimetic. Efficiency and cost-effectiveness may indeed represent the coinage of public justification for many organizations; accordingly, no one should be surprised to find that innovations are presented in such terms. But often there is nothing remotely like clear-cut evidence available to reflect on the cost-effectiveness of any particular innovation.

The best substitute for such evidence, for public consumption, may be to demonstrate that one's own organization displays the same publicly-visible features as other organizations of the same kind. Thus, in universities, for example, one finds the development of such parallel features as core curricula, women's studies departments, and endowed chairs. Whether these institutional features are precisely more cost-effective than various institutional alternatives is perhaps an unanswerable question. But it is clear that their presence helps keep up an indispensable appearance that the university in question is acting like other universities to which it would like to be compared. The example is easily extended to other organizations and other forms of innovation.

Obviously there are significant differences in the views of Kling and Iacono, Ellul, and the New Institutionalists. But for present purposes, their similarities are more important. All three of these share a profound skepticism of any strictly economic account of the auspices of computerization. Whatever the deep forces underlying the press to computerize, all three suggest that these are not apt to be consciously known or directly professed by the actors involved. Instead, these forces arise from diffuse, culturally-entrenched, and unexamined convictions that computing offers solutions to virtually any problem in organization and management—if only decision-makers are far-seeing enough to grasp them. Consequently, for all versions of this skeptical vision, the idea that the extension of computing justifies itself according to any rigorous cost-benefit accounting simply reflects the sham of appearance.

Some Cases from our Interviews

These alternative theoretical views are at least suggestive in relation to our study. And here it helps matters that this study offers something not available in most economists' investigations of computerization: detailed interview data from our site visits and discussions with managers about their actual experiences with computerization. By considering the fine detail of informants' reports of what they did, and what they intended to accomplish in doing so, we may draw some further insight into the ingredients of computerization.

One conclusion that we definitely do *not* draw from these interviews is that classic economic cost-benefit assessment never shapes computing adoption in these cases. On the contrary, our interviews have yielded some detailed accounts that appear to fit that model well. Consider, for example, an application whose adoption was described to us in some detail at a wholesale grocery distributor employing about 500. We had learned in our telephone interview in 1994 that this establishment had recently provided its sales staff with hand-held computers for use by sales representatives in reporting sales to the head office. When we returned for a site interview, our informant explained that the old, paper-based system had indeed been a bottleneck for this company.

Under the old system, he reported, each salesperson would carry paper order sheets around to each store he visited, and check off various items and quantities. At the end of his day, he would have a sheaf of papers representing orders from all his clients. These orders would then have to be telephoned to the parent company, where clerical staff would take them down. Taking these orders over the phone and typing them for further processing took most of the time of five clerical workers. Another big allocation of time went to correcting errors in orders that were discovered during deliveries. These corrections were used to update billing so invoices would be accurate. Since there were some forty-four sales representatives, each had to be assigned a specific time of day to telephone his orders. But this requirement caused problems, in that some telephone orders ran over the allotted time and into the times allocated to other representatives. In other cases, those on the road found themselves unable to locate a telephone at the time designated for transmitting orders.

Now sales representatives enter each customer's orders on a handheld computer before leaving the premises. At the end of their rounds, at any time before 4:00 AM of the following day, they connect their computer by modem to the front office, and the orders are transmitted electronically. At the front office, the receiving computer then automatically prints out "pick tickets" that are in turn provided to delivery drivers the next morning, thus circumventing the need for clerical work. The drivers use these tickets to get the ordered items from the warehouse for delivery the next day. The "pick tickets" prepared in this way are available at 6:30 AM, rather than 10:00 AM under the old system, thus giving the drivers an earlier start on their routes. Our informant reported that the rate of errors in these orders had been reduced by forty percent in the new system.

The initial cost of the hand-held computers, as reported to us, was about $40,000; new computer hardware for the front office cost about $20,000. A fee of $1000 per month is paid to an outside contractor to maintain the system. Against these costs, the firm has eliminated three of the five clerical positions that used to be required to process orders. The yearly labor costs to the company for these three staff alone totaled more than the $60,000 initial investment.

From all indications, the computerization of the ordering process appears to have been cost-effective. But note some features of this application not found in all cases of computer adoption. First, the new activity "maps" almost isomorphically on the one it replaced. That is, the computerized order-entry system does almost exactly what the old system did, thus affording relatively direct comparison between the two—in terms of such matters as dollar costs and rates of errors. We feel that only a minority of applications in our sample, if closely examined, would offer such direct equivalence.

The point is important, because it raises issues central to any assessment of the cost-effectiveness or rationality of computerization. Standard economic thinking, after all, posits that decision-makers weigh specific computerization measures, more or less accurately, against their alternatives for accomplishing comparable ends. But it appears to us that many decisions to computerize are not framed in terms of such clear-cut comparisons. Often, for example, computerization coincides with redefinitions of the tasks involved, so that the "before" and "after" are difficult to compare in cost-effectiveness terms. In such cases, there were numerous accounts in which decision-makers had apparently proceeded on the conviction that computerization simply *had* to be a progressive step—without anyone's being in a position to make exact cost-effectiveness judgments.

Consider, for instance, the two restaurants in our sample that had computerized their communications between the dining room and kitchen. Under the new arrangement, waiters and waitresses could place no orders except through several computer terminals scattered around the dining room, and all diners' checks were prepared electronically on the basis of these orders. These systems were said to reduce otherwise endemic disputes between servers and kitchen staff over what was ordered and when. They were also said to be justified as means of preventing scams against the house, in which diners received dishes that were not written up on any order slip and rewarded the serving staff with a significant tip. Against these benefits, the computerized systems had certain rigidities. For example, they did not permit the server to convey any special instructions as to how the diner wished his or her meal prepared—though we imagine that this did not prevent the server from respectfully accepting such instructions. Thus, presumably, there was some loss in diner satisfaction.

Cost-effectiveness judgments on this innovation must certainly have been problematic from the standpoint of those who made the decision to adopt. Disputes over orders between kitchen and dining room staff were obviously unpleasant to everyone; but how would one measure the actual losses occasioned by such disputes in dollars-and-cents terms? Nor was the maitre d' we interviewed at one of the sites certain that the restaurant had been victimized by diners who received food for which they did not pay; here the system mainly appeared to be a precaution against the possibility of such loss in the future. Finally, it is very difficult to say how one could realistically assess the cost to the restaurant of any dissatisfaction to diners as a result of the (presumably undisclosed) inability of the system to convey their special wishes about the preparation of their food.

We do not mean that the judgments mentioned here are meaningless or unworthy of management concern from a cost-benefit standpoint. But we see no realistic means at the disposal of decision-makers to make them in any authoritative way. The costs of doing so, both in terms of gathering relevant data and developing the analytical tools for their analysis, would far outstrip the resources of most of the organizations in our sample. In the absence of such authoritative bases for cost-effectiveness judgments, it is easy to imagine that the extension of computing is borne largely on a diffuse tide of cultural optimism that computing simply represents "a better way."

Our interviews yielded many indications that such diffuse confidence indeed plays a role in the expansion of computing. In one of the establishments, a general contractor specializing in public works construction, the owner-manager spoke of technological innovation as "the thing to do," even if specific cost-savings could not be anticipated in advance of adoption. He cited, by way of example, the acquisition of a fax machine, which he was sure had paid for itself in terms of fees that would otherwise have to be paid for messenger service, although other principals in the firm had initially questioned the need for it. He applied the same sort of blanket justification to word processing, which the firm had acquired for office use between our 1985 and 1993 interviews. We asked in some detail about the experience of the company with word processing.

The informant reported himself satisfied with the adoption of word processing. Asked as to the repercussions of adoption on the life of the establishment, he identified the main effect as reduction of the amount of secretaries' time spent looking for mis-filed paperwork. We asked whether a dollar value could be ascribed this benefit. The response was negative. The secretaries, our informant noted, were paid the same whether they located correspondence and other files readily or not; with word processing, they probably just had more leisure time at the office, which they spent "reading newspapers or on the phone [in personal calls]." Nor did the informant feel that his firm did any greater volume of correspondence after the addition of word processing.

We find this account revealing; certainly it parallels a variety of others provided by informants in these interviews, both as regards word processing and other forms of innovation. One need not conclude from this story that adoption of word processing in this company was an inept managerial step. Addition of word processing apparently lowered the level of stress in the office; probably it also increased the job satisfaction of secretaries. Managers may quite plausibly consider such benefits worth the modest expense. But one would not expect the effects of such innovation to show up in any analysis of profitability of the firm as a whole.

Close attention to informants' accounts shows many other contexts in which relations between the addition of computing and employment and productivity are subtle or problematic. In this same general contracting company, an early computing application reported in the first wave of interviews in 1985 was the firm's CPM— for "Critical Path Method." This application, in wide use in the construction industry, charts the progress of construction projects in a series of timelines showing what kinds and amounts of work are to be completed at different phases of a contract. These plans are prepared in advance of jobs, and up-dated as the job unfolds, so that discrepancies between schedule and actual progress can readily be noted. In many projects, payments to subcontractors are geared to the progress in their work as recorded on the CPM.

The CPM, then, represents a potential management tool for monitoring of subcontractors' work by the general contractor—and for monitoring the work of the general contractor by the client. Our informant in this company reported that the original reason for acquiring the CPM was to satisfy inflexible client requirements that firms bidding on public-works projects have such capabilities. Given the kind of work that the firm was performing at this stage, he noted, the CPM was of no utility at all, since the judgments on timing and cost that it afforded could as well have been accomplished by simple mental or written reckoning. In this respect, the implication was, the CPM was actually an unproductive investment economically— though formally necessary for the firm to gain access to contracts.

The only real justification for the system where this firm was concerned, the informant observed, was that it enabled public officials to "cover their behinds" with a show of computerized rationality in the supervision of the contracts they let.

Here, therefore, is an ironic insight into some of the forces driving computerization. In order to burnish a public image of economic and administrative rationality, an investment in computing was required that in fact took time and money away from other, potentially more productive uses within the company. Surely this account resonates with the models of institutional change suggested by the New Institutionalists.

But there is an additional twist to the account of this application. During the last several years, our informant explained, the contractor had grown and the projects that it had won had become larger and more complicated. As one result, it had added a new staff member—a civil engineer, whose sole responsibility was to prepare CPM's for bids and to chart work on the CPM when those bids resulted in contracts. But the informant reported that management no longer considered the CPM a useless imposition. For the more complicated projects now being carried out, the CPM actually justified itself by enabling the firm to control costs and coordinate work on a scale that would otherwise be impossible. Asked if the firm would continue to use the CPM if it were no longer required to do so, our informant unhesitatingly answered in the affirmative.

* * *

Accounts like this typify what we see as a widespread feature of computing adoption—the absence of exact standards by which to judge whether a particular innovation can be considered cost-effective, either prospectively or (sometimes) retrospectively. We stress that we do not mean by this that judgements involved are often manifestly *ir*rational—that is, that they could be known in advance as likely to result in *diminished* cost-effectiveness. We simply mean that, with information practically available to decision-makers, definitive decisions along these lines were bound to be problematic. Under these circumstances, we hold, diffuse cultural assumptions on computing—myths, in the non-pejorative sense—may play a potent role.

One sort of evidence to support this position derives from data on an aspect of computerization not yet discussed—the role of computer applications that are *dropped*. We have shown that growth in computing is clearly the norm during the time period covered by this study. The typical organization in our panel added some 1.5 applications between 1985 and 1993. This finding did not come as a surprise to us. But we were impressed to note how rare it is for applications to be reported discontinued; we find a total of only six such cases, against a total of 351 applications reported by all eighty-two panel establishments in 1993.

We can think of two broad interpretations of such a finding. On the one hand, computing adoptions may be so highly cost-effective that they rarely fail to achieve the savings intended in their adoption. But the alternate interpretation is that the standards by which the worth of computing applications are judged are simply too diffuse to admit of rigorous negative judgments.

Occasionally, judgments of the first sort are in fact made. This was the case with a computer application reported in 1985 by a creamery and wholesaler of milk products—a series of hand-held computers intended to accomplish many of the same tasks addressed by the hand-held computers used by salespersons in the food wholesaling company described above. The 1985 interviewer described these as follows:

> Since the drivers often take orders from their customers directly while they are delivering the milk (they take the next day's order), the firm decided to get some hand-held computers. The driver can punch in on the computer the different items that the customer wants. He can also print out a receipt for customers who are paying in cash... When the driver comes in at the end of the day, he hooks up the computer to a modem and the orders are read into the computer and printed out. (#267)

As far we could tell from this account, the addition of these devices sounded like an entirely rational business decision. But in our subsequent 1993 interview at this same establishment, we learned that the hand-held computers had been discarded; the ordering process was once again being done by conventional means. The equipment had kept breaking down. Further, management reported that on reconsideration, the orders recorded through the system had never really been sufficiently variable to warrant using the hand-held devices. Unlike the situation at the wholesale grocery described above, orders came from a relatively small number of customers whose needs did not change greatly from one order to the next. Two additional clerical staff were reported to have been added to handle the communications previously transmitted by computer.

This account would not strike us as remarkable, were it not so rare in our sample. We have to wonder why such unsuccessful experiments in computerization are not reported much more frequently. True, many computing arrangements represent "sunk costs" once in place, such that the cost of keeping them operating is lower than that of instating them in the first place. A word processing program, for example, that is rarely used but remains loaded on the office PC might well still be reported to our interviewers as an existing application. Indeed, we suspect that such reports are more likely, to the extent that those who adopted the applications in question are anxious about having made what may in retrospect appear as a cost-ineffective innovation. But in most instances, such scrutiny after the fact probably just does not take place—if indeed it is possible. For a computerized system of communications between dining room and kitchen in a restaurant, or a computerized system for tracking job orders through their stages of production, or any number of other purposes, criteria of success and failure may be far from clear-cut.

Interpretations: Quality Improvement and Quality Degradation

Even among economists, ambiguous findings on productivity growth have inspired reflection on not-exclusively-economic considerations in the adoption of new technologies. In a long and thoughtful study of computing and slackened productivity growth, Martin Neil Bailly and Robert J. Gordon are moved to consider some scenarios clearly antipathetic to efficiency models of computing adoption. Computing, they speculate,

> may encourage waste and inefficiency. Computers provide a flow of services that companies do not know how to value. White-collar groups sometimes measure their performance on the basis of the amount of information or paperwork they generate rather than on its value to a company. (1988, p. 391)

This and other scenarios of computer adoption entertained by these authors, it seems to us, could as well be put forward by representatives of the New Institutionalists.

Some economists, including Bailly and Gordon, stress that computing and similar innovations may bring what they term "quality improvements" (p. 377) that are undetectable by formal cost-benefit reckoning. Thus, for example, computerization may make reserving hotel rooms and airline flights much more convenient, though these benefits to customers may not show up on any ledger sheet.

No doubt such uncosted improvements do occur, but the role they play in economists' arguments raises problems. For one thing, it will not do to imagine that all the unmeasured quality repercussions of computerization are "improvements." As always, one must ask "for whom, and in what interest?" Many uses of the new technology, though perhaps desirable from *somebody's* standpoint, clearly result in inconvenience and degradation of services to those dealing with the organizations involved—for example, the proliferation of automated user-unfriendly telephone answering systems whose main effect seems to be to insulate organizations from attending to callers' questions and other needs.

These possibilities raise theoretical issues. Economic views of computerization—and nearly anything else—can be applied so as to make it almost unthinkable that investment is guided by any considerations other than classic cost-benefit rationality. This issue arises, for example, in the writing of Erik Brynjolfsson, author of a number of studies strongly upholding the cost-effectiveness of investment in computing. In an article entitled "The Intangible Costs and Benefits of Computer Investments," Brynjolfsson and Yang examine relations between companies' investment in computer capital and market valuations of those companies' stock. "Strikingly," they write, "each dollar of computer capital is associated with over $15 of market value" (1998, p. 10). This finding is indeed striking, and also apparently inconsistent with economic theory, which would suggest that much more investment should occur than is already the case, given the returns that computer capital apparently yields. They quote Robert Gordon's remark, "if IT [information technology] has excess returns, what is the hidden force that prevents greater investments?" (1998, p. 10).

Brynjolfsson and Yang's explanation for this seeming anomaly is what they call "intangible costs and benefits" of computing. These consist of the complex organizational learning and restructuring associated with computerization (costs) and the commensurate benefits accruing to companies endowed with the resulting capabilities. They write:

> While these tangible assets are overlooked in standard production functions, they may be just as real as other assets in their ability to generate value. In other words, the output increases associated with computer capital are not necessarily "excess" re-

turns, but rather reflect returns on a collection of partially unmeasured assets. (1998, p. 10)

This line of reasoning of course readily reconciles the seeming disproportion between measurable investment in companies' computing resources and their market value. The question is, is such thinking at all falsifiable? How do we know, for example, that the high valuations ascribed by markets to highly computerized companies have any specific relation to the uncosted investments that go into computerization? And how do we know that the value ascribed by markets to highly computerized companies results from capacities imparted by the technology independent of any mystique conferred by the cultural halo of computing—capacities that would be marketable even under a "veil of ignorance" as to the role played in them by any specific technology.

There can be no doubt that computing does play such an image-enhancing role, and that these public representations may have dollars-and-cents repercussions. We have evidence of this on a small scale from our own interviews. One informant told us, for example, that he preferred to do billing in his small business by computer, because he felt that clients were less likely to disregard a computerized bill than a manually-prepared one. In another interview, a manager in a small, suburban nursery business reported having computerized the process of estimating new landscaping jobs. The informant affirmed his belief that this step enhanced productivity but also noted, in the words of the interviewer,

> the upscale clientele [of this nursery] demand a professional accounting of costs. The computerized account record looks slicker and is used as a selling tool.

Note that we hardly deny the potential cost-effectiveness of computing purely as an enhancer of the public image of organizational capabilities. We simply wish to underline what we consider an important conceptual distinction between computing-as-a-source-of-capabilities-demonstrably-valuable-in-themselves and computing-as-a-marker.

The larger point is that there may be many sociologically convincing accounts of the motives driving computerization—as viewed from the standpoint of private-sector decision-makers who actually order the new systems. Computing may be seen, more or less accurately, as a cost-effective investment. But the success of such investment decisions—when they are deemed to succeed—may derive from all sorts of processes other than increased efficiency in the task-performances to which they are ostensibly applied. Rather than making it possible produce more widgets or services per day, for example, computing may serve to impress important customers with the progressive profile of the organization.

Finally, further complicating such assessments is the question of whether computing represents *investment* or *consumption*—or perhaps some rich and complex mingling of the two. Given the role of computing in the cultural iconography of our time, it would hardly be surprising to find that computerization represents a kind of luxury good for decision-makers in all sorts of organizations. In this view, managers in private-sector establishments who have the opportunity will be likely to purchase the trappings of organizational success, in the form of new computing systems, if only to broadcast to themselves and to the their social environment that they are doing well. Such opportunities will obviously be more widely available to organizations with generous cash flows—a fact that could itself yield strong associations between profitability and computerization reported by some researchers. But if computerization represents "consumption" in these cases, as we have tried to show, such consumption may also offer certain practical benefits to the organizations involved.

Conclusions

No one doubts that computing is at the center of some of today's most multifarious and far-reaching forms of social change. But doubts and debates evidently proliferate over the exact nature of these changes and the processes by which they are occurring. Based on evidence from the interviews reported here, we readily accept that computing has the capability to accomplish all sorts of work done in organizations more quickly and more efficiently than by conventional means—in ways that would matter, even if the role of computing in them were concealed from all concerned. But, is it indeed these characteristics that drive specific processes of social change? Or is the agent of change the *mythology* associated with the technology—the conviction that anything accomplished by computing *must* be more effective, more efficient, or more progressive?

It is all-but-universally recognized that countless socially important beliefs and assumptions must be counted as true if they are widely accepted as such. Sociologists have coined catchphrases like "situations defined as real" and "self-fulfilling prophecies" to point to such beliefs. The term *myth* conveys many of the same connotations. Technologies certainly have mythic qualities, we have sought to show, among many other socially consequential characteristics.

To assess how and why technological change matters, we need to ask not only how people think and feel about the technology, but also about constraints on human experience imposed by non-human characteristics of those same technologies. The theoretical possibility of controlled nuclear explosions might have been conceived as a myth in the minds of nuclear researchers and military planners in the 1930s and early '40s, for example. That myth, if we are to call it such, generated a feverish array of social processes—though initially much more secretive ones than any connected with computing today. But once the first nuclear detonation occurred, the force of that technology in human affairs clearly derived from more than just its mythic status. At some point, treating any technology as *only* a myth misses something essential about its input in human affairs.

For students of computing, no task is more urgent than that of disentangling these aspects in its social role. The pursuit of such disentanglement can be maddeningly complex—as Paul Attewell demonstrates in his review of a number of studies of computing and productivity. Commenting on an ingenious analysis by Pentland (1989) of computerization of IRS agents' work, Attewell notes,

> Pentland found striking discrepancies between the self-report findings and analyses of objective measures of the same agents' work. None of the computerized features was associated with increased productivity measured objectively, and several were associated with lower productivity. The implication is that agents' efforts at improving quality through computers undermined their productivity.
>
> Nor was there a 'real' effect of computer use on objective quality of work. Pentland found a widespread belief among the IRS staff that the use of word processing was more authoritative and would lead taxpayers to accept an unfavorable audit result. But this belief proved unfounded when tested with objective data. Agents used more word processing in big cases and in contested cases, in order to bolster their sense of professionalism and credibility, but it had no effect on the outcome. (Attewell 1994, p. 30.)

Here, as in some of the material from our interviews, what people *believed* about the power of computing demonstrably outstripped the verifiable capabilities of the technology. But this conclusion should hardly translate into generic skepticism regarding the potential contribution of computing to change in efficiency and employment levels. The only reasonable assumption is that the mythology of computing and its instrumental usefulness interact in shaping the ways in which organizations work.

Indeed, we perceive in this mixture of mythic and other processes the elements of a useful sociological model—a model accounting for the sustained proliferation of computing in the face of evidence of its effects that is, at the least, ambiguous. In this view, a few well-publicized success stories sustain a pervasive public optimism and legitimacy concerning the cost-effectiveness of computerization. These high-visibility paradigms in turn provide a selective filter through which *all* computing innovations are subsequently viewed. Thus prospects for computerization with highly ambiguous cost-benefit justifications nevertheless receive "the benefit of the doubt" in the minds of management decision-makers. Experiences in which computerization brings little or no demonstrable cost-benefit advantage simply do not figure in the public's—or managers'—overall view of computerization.

In a much-noted article, Paul David (1990) has compared the reception of computing to that of steam power in the early phases of the industrial revolution. He points out that, while the principles that ultimately made steam a highly productive technology were known early on, its measurable aggregate effects took decades to register. Something similar may have occurred at the end of the twentieth century. In retrospect, this period may appear to economic historians as one in which the principles by which computing might pay for itself were widely recognized, but only rarely realized in ways with direct cost-benefit significance. In any event, for the private-sector decision makers surveyed in this study, we sense that computing appears as a kind of generic *good thing*—so much as to overwhelm vast uncertainties as to what measurable difference any specific computing innovation will make in the balance sheet of the enterprise.

Appendix 5.1

Pearson Correlation Coefficients for Relevant Variables (N=82)[a].

	1	2	3	4	5	6	7	8	9	10	11	12	13	14	15	16	17	18	19	20	21
1. 1985 Staff	1																				
2. 1993 Staff	.91*	1																			
3. Percent Change in Staffing	.02	.31*	1																		
4. 1985 Computing	.27*	.26*	-.05	1																	
5. 1993 Computing	.20	.24*	.04	.65*	1																
6. Percent Change in Computing	-.18	-.11	.17	-.55*	.15	1															
7. 1985 Sales	.15	.23*	.15	.29*	.23*	-.07	1														
8. 1993 Sales	.48*	.61*	.20	.34*	.33*	-.06	.34*	1													
9. Percent Change in Sales	.11	.13	.10	.06	-.05	-.37	-.09	.45*	1												
10. Percent Change in Sales/Staff	.08	.04	-.10	.07	-.08	-.12	-.13	.36*	.96*	1											
11. Area: Manhattan	.09	.05	-.09	.12	.03	-.15	-.05	.08	-.10	-.05	1										
12. Area: Brooklyn/Queen	-.08	-.03	.03	-.03	.03	-.1	-.08	.09	.18	.15	-.46*	1									
13. Area: Nassau/Suffolk County	-.01	-.03	.06	-.09	-.06	.04	.12	-.16	-.07	-.09	-.53*	-.50*	1								
14. SIC: Construction	.00	-.05	-.06	-.02	.04	.12	-.05	-.12	-.01	.05	.06	.08	-.13	1							
15. SIC: Discrete Manufacturing	-.12	-.08	-.04	.00	.09	.09	.01	.11	-.04	-.04	-.02	.08	-.05	-.14	1						
16. SIC: Process Manufacturing	.13	.06	-.09	-.12	.03	.08	-.05	-.06	-.07	-.06	-.10	.02	.08	-.10	-.11	1					
17. SIC: Transport/Communic/Utilit	.06	-.02	-.11	.10	.14	-.03	-.02	-.05	-.04	-.03	-.16	-.03	.18	-.08	-.08	-.06	1				
18. SIC: Wholesale	-.21	-.15	.11	.03	-.02	-.15	-.05	-.08	-.07	-.08	-.04	.05	-.01	-.17	-.17	-.13	-.10	1			
19. SIC: Retail	-.00	.06	.05	-.23*	-.12	.22*	-.05	.12	.06	.02	-.02	-.07	.09	-.16	-.16	-.12	-.10	-.20	1		
20. SIC: Finance/Real Estate/Insur	.23*	.19	-.07	.22*	.09	-.18	.36*	.23*	.26*	.28*	.07	-.11	.04	-.11	-.11	-.09	-.07	-.14	-.13	1	
21. SIC: Services	.02	.03	.10	.07	-.10	-.15	-.08	-.12	-.06	-.09	.13	-.03	-.10	-.20	-.20	-.15	-.12	-.24*	-.23*	-.16	1

[a] Panel study firms, controlling for exogenous change; *(p<.05)

Appendix 5.2

Effects of Computing Growth on Staffing
Levels Among Panel Organizations, 1985-1993 (N=82).

	Percent Change in Staffing, 1985-1993			Odds of Increasing Staff 1985-1993	
	Decreased or No Change		Increased	Odds Ratio (95% CI)	
	N	%	N	%	Unadjusted	Adjusted
Percent Change in Computing 1985-1993						
Increased more than mean	14	46.7	16	53.3	2.82 (1.11-7.18)*	8.57 (2.01-36.67)**
Less than mean	37	71.2	15	28.8	1.00	1.00
Percent Change in Sales 1985-1993						
Increased more than mean	8	42.1	11	57.9	2.96 (1.03-8.48)*	4.18 (1.15-15.17)*
Less than mean	43	68.3	20	31.7	1.00	1.00
1985 Level of Computing						
Higher than mean	24	61.5	15	38.5	1.06 (0.43-2.58)	1.42 (0.42-4.85)
Lower than mean	27	62.8	16	37.2	1.00	1.00
1985 Sales Revenue						
Higher than mean	14	50.0	14	50.0	2.18 (0.85-5.56)	2.87 (0.89-9.24)+
Lower than mean	37	68.5	17	31.5	1.00	1.00
1985 Total Site Employees						
Higher than mean	17	56.7	13	43.3	1.44 (0.58-3.63)	2.82 (0.82-9.62)+
Lower than mean	34	65.4	18	34.6	1.00	1.00
Standard Industrial Code (SIC)[a]						
Construction/Transport/Utilities	11	78.6	3	21.4	0.33 (0.07-1.57)	0.27 (0.05-1.54)
Manufacturing	12	75.0	4	25.0	0.41 (0.10-1.71)	0.33 (0.06-1.73)
Wholesale/Service	17	53.1	15	46.9	1.08 (0.35-3.31)	2.11 (0.52-8.57)
Retail/Financ/Insurance	11	55.0	9	45.0	1.00	1.00
-2 Log Likelihood						85.18
Goodness-of-Fit X^2 [Hosmer-Lemeshow]:						3.28, df=8, p=0.916
Model Chi-Square						23.57, df=8, p=0.003
N						82

CI: Confidence Interval
+p<.10, *p<.05, **p<.01, ***p<.001
[a] SIC: Standard Industrial Classification (Reference Group is Retail/Financial/Insurance)

Appendix 5.3

Effects of Computing Growth on Efficiency Among
Panel Organizations, 1985-1993 (N=82).

	Percent Change in Efficiency, 1985-1993				Odds of Increased Efficiency 1985-1993	
	Low/No Increase		High Increase		Odds Ratio (95% CI)	
	N	%	N	%	Unadjusted	Adjusted
Percent Change in Computing 1985-1993						
Increased more than mean	19	63.3	11	36.7	0.79 (0.31-1.99)	0.47 (0.14-1.66)
Less than mean	30	57.7	22	42.3	1.00	1.00
Percent Change in Sales 1985-1993						
Increased more than mean	3	15.8	16	84.2	14.43 (3.73-55.82)***	16.70 (3.76-74.08)***
Less than mean	46	73.0	17	27.0	1.00	1.00
1985 Level of Computing						
Higher than mean	24	61.5	15	38.5	0.87 (0.36-2.11)	0.99 (0.30-3.26)
Lower than mean	25	58.1	18	41.9	1.00	1.00
1985 Sales Revenue						
Higher than mean	22	78.6	6	21.4	0.27 (0.10-0.78)*	0.28 (0.08-1.00)*
Lower than mean	27	50.0	27	50.0	1.00	1.00
1985 Total Site Employees						
Higher than mean	18	60.0	12	40.0	0.98 (0.39-2.46)	0.67 (0.20-2.25)
Lower than mean	31	59.6	21	40.4	1.00	1.00
Standard Industrial Code (SIC)[a]						
Construction/Transport/Utilities	8	57.1	6	42.9	0.92 (0.23-3.63)	0.86 (0.15-4.92)
Manufacturing	10	62.5	6	37.5	0.73 (0.19-2.81)	0.69 (0.14-3.43)
Wholesale/Service	20	62.5	12	37.5	0.73 (0.24-2.28)	0.58 (0.15-2.30)
Retail/Financ/Insurance	11	55.0	9	45.0	1.00	1.00
-2 Log Likelihood						83.26
Goodness-of-Fit X^2 [Hosmer-Lemeshow]:						7.79, df=8, p=0.454
Model Chi-Square						27.28, df=8, p=0.001
N						82

CI: Confidence Interval

+p<.10, *p<.05, **p<.01, ***p<.001

[a] SIC: Standard Industrial Classification (Reference Group is Retail/Financial/Insurance)

6

Management and Structure

In all the commentary on computing, one of the most durable themes has been its "revolutionary" repercussions for the ways in which organization are managed. Observers expect the mindsets of managers, and hence the most basic strategies and possibilities of organizational action, to be radically challenged, upset, or reversed. Such profound changes are bound, it is said, to result in far-reaching alterations of the institutional *form* of organizations.

Commonalities in these prophecies soon become apparent. Computing begins its revolutionary revamping of management, according to many commentaries, through its effects on *authority*. Shoshanna Zuboff's words are exemplary here. The impetus to change that she identifies has to do with relations between knowledge and organizational action:

> The shifting grounds of knowledge invite managers to recognize the emergent demands for intellective skills and develop a learning environment in which such skills can develop. The very recognition contains a threat to managerial authority, which depends in part upon control over the organization's knowledge base. A commitment to intellective skill development is likely to be hampered when an organization's division of labor continuously replenishes the felt necessity of imperative control. Managers who must prove and defend their own legitimacy do not easily share knowledge or engage in inquiry. Workers who feel the requirements of subordination are not enthusiastic learners. New roles cannot emerge without new structures to support them. (1988, p. 191)

The detail of Zuboff's argument is distinctive, but the form has many parallels among commentaries on the subject. Something about computerization, it is posited, alters the *micro-sociology* of organizations—the content of the information exchanged, for example, or the patterns of communication, or discretion over certain decisions. These *molecular* changes in turn trigger far-reaching rearrangements of familiar institutions, hierarchies, and divisions of labor. That is, they change patterns of who manages whom, of how managers communicate, or indeed of what kinds of work need to be carried out.

Very commonly, these prognostications (including Zuboff's) have to do with stratification—that is, with the collegial versus hierarchical character of organizations. Another eminent voice to this effect is that of Peter Drucker. Once the effects of computing within organizations sink in, Drucker believes, management will undergo vast transformation:

> [A]s soon as a company takes the first tentative steps from data to information, its decision processes, management structure, and even the way its work gets done begin to be transformed...
>
> ...Almost immediately, it becomes clear that both the numbers of management levels and the number of managers can be sharply cut. The reason is straightforward: it turns out that whole layers of management neither make decisions nor lead. Instead, their main, if not their only, function is to serve as "relays"—human boosters for the faint, unfocused signals that pass for communication in the traditional pre-information organization...
>
> Because the "players" in an information-based organization are specialists, they cannot be told how to do their work. There are probably few orchestra conductors who could coax even one note out of a French horn, let alone show the horn player how to do it. But the conductor can focus the horn player's skill and knowledge on the musicians' joint performance. And this focus is what the leaders of an information-based business must be able to achieve. (Drucker 1988, pp. 45-49)

Like Zuboff, Drucker thus sees computerizing organizations as increasingly egalitarian, even collegial, once otiose layers of middle management fall away.

These two authors articulate the upbeat version of this argument. Perhaps inevitably, they have their antithesis in darker visions. In these views, computing is bound to render managers more self-sufficient in terms of information, and hence organizations themselves more hierarchical. One version of this view is furnished by Harry Braverman:

> ...the computerization of office accounting procedures further weakens the position of those skilled in the system as a whole, particularly bookkeepers.
>
> Not only bookkeepers, but even the lower grades of management, feel the effects in a similar way. The computer presents management with an enormous temptation to save management time as well as labor time by 'mechanizing' many choices and decisions. It is probably for this reason that Howard C. Carlson, a psychologist employed by General Motors, has said: 'The computer may be to middle management what the assembly line has been to the hourly worker.' (1974, pp. 333-340)

Or, in the words of another commentator, "The office of the future would...leave people in only two roles: bosses and garbage collectors" (Driscoll 1982).

Hierarchies and Job Categories

It seems clear that, in the absence of systematic observation, sweeping forms of *a priori* thinking abound on these matters. But our study can directly assess some empirical implications of these prophecies, simply by comparing the stratification of organizations in the panel before and after computerization. In both the 1985 and 1993 interviews, we asked informants to specify the *levels of management* prevailing in their establishments—the number of distinct layers of order-giving from top management to those who actually direct the performance of work. Table 6.1 shows these comparisons.

Like other empirical investigators on this point (e.g., Laudon and Marr 1995), we find no evidence that computerization has any *net* tendency to render organizations more or less hierarchical. Organizations in the panel were about as likely to reduce as to raise the number of management levels reported from 1985 to 1993. And rapidly computerizing organizations were not essentially different from their less rapidly computerizing counterparts in this respect.

Table 6.1

Change in Management Levels for High Computerization Versus Low Computerization Establishments 1985-1993 (N=80)[a].

Change in MGT Levels 1985-1993	Organizations with High Increase in Computing 1985-1993 (N=30)		Organizations with Low or No Increase in Computing 1985-1993 (N=50)		Analysis	
	%	N	%	N	X^2 (df=2)	p
Rising Hierarchy	36.7	11	28.0	14	0.66	ns
No Change	36.7	11	42.0	21		
Declining Hierarchy	26.7	8	30.0	15		

[a]Two organizations missing due to missing responses for job categories.

ns: Not Significant

Beyond prognostications on management hierarchy *per se*, many commentators have prophesied that computerization would lead to far-reaching changes in the distribution of work roles. Perhaps the most common prediction is that one or another job category will be drastically reduced as its functions are replicated by the machines. Peter Drucker levels this prediction at middle management in the passage quoted above. Some authors have applied the same expectations to other job categories—most frequently, to clerical work.

These predictions are hardly unintuitive, and individual accounts from even our earliest interviews made us inclined to take them seriously. In the previous chapter, we described how management at [231], the wholesale supplier of Hispanic grocery items, had made redundant the work of several secretaries by providing their salesmen with hand-held computers. These devices transmitted orders directly back to the front-office computer, which electronically generated delivery instructions for the company's drivers—thus circumventing the secretaries, who had previously taken down phone orders and typed up the drivers' daily instructions. Most of the secretaries were reported to have lost their jobs as a direct result of this computerization.

We recorded much the same story in our interview with [133], a manufacturers' representative for lighting fixtures and other construction finishing items. This suburban business had a staff of twenty-six at the time of our 1985 interview, including fifteen salespersons and six clerks. At our second interview in 1993, the sales staff had risen to twenty-nine, while clerical staff had sunk to zero. In the intervening years, the company had adopted computing arrangements enabling sales staff to transmit orders electronically to wholesalers. Clerical staff had become entirely redundant.

Clerical workers seem especially likely to be replaced when they serve as "relays" (to use Drucker's term) for information which, it is discovered, can more efficiently be moved by computer. We recorded another instance of this vulnerability at [128], a suburban "practice management" company engaged in billing for physicians and other healthcare providers. This establishment reported a staff of 150 in 1985, declining to 105 in 1993. Most of this decline had resulted from a precipitous drop in clerical employment—the direct result of extensive computerization, our management interlocutor told us.

In 1985, clerical staff at [128] had been largely engaged in highly routine—indeed, almost mind numbing—data entry tasks. The "raw material" for this work was a steady input of medical records from the company's clients, detailing patients seen and treatments provided. Workers transformed these data into mass billings to insurers and other third-party payers. In 1993, our management informant insisted that the volume of such work had increased greatly since 1985, even while the numbers of those carrying it had out plummeted. In the intervening years, it seemed that the hospitals and other organizations generating the charges had begun to computerize their own records, so that their billing information came to [128] in electronic form.

Thus the need to enter all sorts of data, including patients' names, addresses, date of birth, etc., was short-circuited. Instead of having to reenter all these data for each billing, the [128] staff simply added billing requests to the electronic record, and transmitted both electronically to the billed parties. Our interlocutor insisted, in the words of the interviewer, that "despite handling 2-3 times the volume...prior to receiving patient records on magnetic tapes, the firm has reduced staff used for patient record keeping by more than half" (March 16, 1994). Similar staff reductions were reported to have resulted from the installation of an online system for responding to patients' queries on their accounts. Before computerization, customer service representatives could only provide information to patients, accept their requests to change records and transmit requests for change to data entry staff. Under the new system, the same women who answered the phone inquiries could directly enter the computer records and effect changes.

A succession of accounts like this left us inclined to expect that organizations in our sample would show losses of clerical workers as a net "effect" of computerization. We also suspected that management numbers might show similar change. Had such "effects" been present, our panel data should certainly have reflected them, since interviews at both points recorded data both on total staffing and on the distribution of staff across job categories; Appendix 6.1 shows these proportions at the two data points.

But as Table 6.2 shows, the only category whose proportion is altered to any noteworthy extent is that of clerical workers—whose numbers tend to be reduced, but not to a statistically significant level in this bivariate analysis. Further multivariate analysis, shown in Table 6.3, shows that computerization during the period under study does indeed predict decrease in proportion of staff made up

Table 6.2

Change in Distribution of Staff Across Job Categories as a Function of Computerization, 1985-1993 (N=82).

Job Categories	Organizations with High Increase in Computing 1985-1993 (N=30)		Organizations with Low or No Increase in Computing 1985-1993 (N=51)[a]		Analysis	
	Mean Percent Change T1-T2	SD	Mean Percent Change T1-T2	SD	t	p
Total Staff	23.1	70.1	-2.0	60.3	1.71	0.091
Proportion of Total Staff[a]						
Management	24.8	86.5	19.3	55.4	0.35	ns
Professional	7.6	68.9	54.2	350.7	-0.72	ns
Sales	55.3	229.3	339.2	1410.5	-1.41	ns
Clerical	-19.1	37.1	-0.3	46.1	-1.90	0.061
Shop Floor/Warehouse	-17.0	37.6	86.7	543.8	-1.04	ns
Maintenance/Janitorial	77.8	236.1	94.1	422.5	-0.19	ns
Programmers/Computing	18.4	57.4	17.0	105.3	0.07	ns
Other	231.5	660.9	354.9	1096.0	-0.56	ns

SD: Standard Deviation; ns: Not statistically significant.
[a]One organization missing due to missing responses for job categories.

of clerical workers. After controlling for the other variables in the model, organizations showing higher than average increase in computing between 1985 and 1993 *decreased* their proportion of clerical staffing by 26.9%. The level of computing reported in 1985 had almost as strong a relationship to proportion of clerical staff in 1993. No other job category showed such effects under multivariate analysis.

The panel study does, then, give evidence of the role of computerization in reducing the proportion clerical staffing, but no indication in either direction where management or other job categories are concerned. Nevertheless, we believe that categorical conclusions about the "effects" of computerization on any one job category may be oversimplified. If our interviews show anything, it is that the "same" technology may have quite opposite "effects" in different establishments—such that aggregation actually works to

Table 6.3

Effects of Computing Growth and Other Variables on Change in Proportion of Clerical Staffing Within Panel Organizations, 1985-1993 (N=81)[a].

	Percent Change in Proportion of Clerical Staffing, 1985-1993		
Independent variables[b]	b	(se)	Beta
High Percent Change in Computing 1985-1993	-26.9	(10.8)	-0.30*
High Percent Change in Sales 1985-1993	1.2	(11.0)	0.01
1985 Level of Computing	-22.5	(10.5)	-0.26*
1985 Sales Revenue	-4.1	(10.2)	-0.04
1985 Total Site Employees	8.7	(10.4)	0.10
Standard Industrial Classification (SIC)[c]			
Construction/Transport/Utilities	43.2	(14.4)	0.38**
Manufacturing	18.6	(13.9)	0.17
Wholesale/Service	11.5	(12.0)	0.13
Constant	-4.3	(12.7)	0.00
F-Value	2.51, df=8, p=0.018		
R^2	0.218		
N	81		

b: Unstandardized Regression Coefficient; **(se)**: Standard Error; **Beta**: Standardized Regression Coefficient

+p<.10, *p<.05, **p<.01, ***p<.001

[a] One organization missing due to missing response for job categories.

[b] Independent variables dichotomized at their means: 1=Higher than mean, 0=Mean or lower.

[c] SIC: Standard Industrial Classification Reference Group is Retail/Financial/Insurance

obscure a series of interesting and significant processes that may simply cancel each other quantitatively.

Thus some establishments in our study also afford numerous examples of applications associated with *increases* in clerical and other staffing. One such account comes from [247], the upscale Manhattan clothier whose computerized monitoring of buyers' productivity was discussed in Chapter 4. When we returned to this organization for our 1993 interview, we found that it had added a fifth computer application, a kind of master inventory control and accounting operation. This application was reported to have required the addition of five clerical workers—presumably considered by management to be justified on cost-effectiveness grounds, but nevertheless a net gain in staff. Other interviews also registered accounts of applications that triggered marked growth in specific job categories between 1985 and 1993. We see no reason to regard these "effects" of computerization as any less authentic than in cases where applications substitute directly for human labor.

A New Management Structure:
Computerized Organizational Linkages

If our panel data failed consistently to show all the structural changes widely expected to result from computerization, it also unexpectedly revealed the emergence of some structures that we had not anticipated. Notable among these were new institutions of connection and coordination *across* establishments—linkages between organizations formed through computerized communication. These connections took many forms, including ties to customers, suppliers, and government agencies. All in all, we classified some 12.6% of the 230 applications reported in the 1985 panel and 12.0% of the 351 applications in the 1993 panel as involving some form of direct computerized coordination of these kinds.

The simplest of these connections involved one establishment's making available some elements of its own computer records to one or more outside organization. One establishment reporting such an innovation was [12], a worldwide air courier service providing pickup and international delivery of small packages. In the early 1980s, [12's] managers decided that too much staff time was being devoted to tracing the status of shipments—in response to requests either from shippers or from intended recipients. Their solution was to launch a computerized job-tracking application, in which each step in the handling of each shipment required an electronic "signature" from the staff person responsible. The effect was to create an online compendium of data on the current status of each order, available for immediate access by [12] staff.

A later refinement of this application extended its use to the customers themselves. Thus, instead of calling [12] staff for information about how far along a package was in the shipment process, customers could log onto the [12] computer and obtain the same data for themselves. We encountered at least one similar solution elsewhere in the study—a moving and storage company affiliated with a larger national company of the same kind. Here, too, the linkage effectively brought the customers involved directly "inside" the organization by providing the same computerized job tracking data available to staff.

Such simple arrangements obviously involve minimal qualitative change in the workings of the organizations. But as computerized linkages evolve, they may begin to change organizational agendas and repertoires, including the division of labor between linked organizations. One such case from our panel was [126], an importer, manufacturer, and wholesaler of sunglasses. The retail customers of this company sell the glasses mainly on display racks of the sort often encountered in drug stores. For [126], reordering had been a weak link in its business. Many retailers apparently did not reorder promptly; when they did, they failed to select the specific products that [126] was convinced were most likely to sell.

In response, [126] developed a computerized strategy for taking the entire reordering process out of the hands of the retailers. In the most sophisticated version of this process, a nationally known discount drug chain went online with [126]; as related by our interviewer:

> [126] provides a terminal and modem hook-up to [its] computer. [The retailer] simply enters their inventory of sunglasses each week. [126]...by comparing this year's sales and last year's sales generates a purchase order and ships [the retailer] the appropriate number of sunglasses. [The retailer]...does not have to do anything but enter inventory. [126] provides a liberal return policy for over-ordering.

The interviewer goes on to note that smaller retailers follow a similar procedure, without the computer hookup. Salespersons visit these establishments and record current inventory, which [126] then replenishes, according to its own computerized algorithm for maximizing future sales.

This arrangement corresponds to what some business analysts call *strategic information systems*—computerization programs aimed to exert competitive advantage over other potential suppliers (Wiseman 1988; Clemons and Row 1988). By actually taking over a portion of the retailer's work in reordering and restocking display space, [126] in effect made its role more difficult to replicate, while controlling the choice of what new merchandise to display. One might say that a system like this succeeds by altering the division of labor between organizations, creating a dependency desirable from the standpoint of [126].

This is not the only panel organization reporting computerized linkage of this kind. Another was [163], a suburban business with a staff of 225, mainly warehouse workers. This rather unusual company neither makes nor sells any product of its own. Instead, it specializes in maintaining inventories of some 6,000 of what it calls

"SKU's," or "stock-keeping units," for the companies selling them, and shipping these items on request. Thus a toy manufacturer, for example, might have hundreds of items held at this location, ready to be shipped by [163] on request. Orders for these goods come electronically from the wholesalers and from their clients (i.e., retailers intending to sell the warehoused items). Asked about the reasons for acquiring this system, their vice president replied that the company had adopted it

> to make themselves more competitive...several large retailers prefer to do their ordering [by computer] because it cuts down on paperwork and *won't do business with firms that can't provide access to this type of system* [emphasis added]...[the vice president claims] that he would prefer all orders to come in through an electronic medium as this greatly reduces the amount of paperwork that [163] has to manage as well.

Here, too, we see computing opening the way to an altered division of labor, and a new juxtaposition of interests, between the linked organizations. As in other strategic information systems described in the literature, [163] used this system to create sales reports and other information for the benefit of its clients.

Clemons and Row (1988) describe the strategic information system that they studied—a pharmaceutical supplier to independent retail drugstores—as shaped by sharp competitive pressures from manufacturers of drugs, as well as from other suppliers. In both the cases from our panel, the systems were also adopted with an eye to potential competition, though [126] seemed to be acting to *forestall* competition, whereas [163] seems to have been reacting to immediate threats of loss of business.

In other cases, computerized linkage between organizations appeared to set the stage for more overt manifestations of power relations. Two establishments in our panel were nursing homes; like most such institutions, their billings went to third-party payers, usually agencies of the State of New York. Here computerization appeared to have provided the opportunity for the state to micromanage the care that patients were receiving.

Just prior to our 1985 interviews, for instance, New York had begun to require that nursing homes and similar institutions submit their billings by computer. In the words of our interviewer, the decision of [124] to computerize

> was really compelled by the fact that the state had begun to require bills for each patient...[the home] had to bill the state for each patient each month—a fourfold increase in paperwork. Moreover, the state has very complicated rate payment criteria,

and figuring out how much nursing time will be required (and how much will be allowed by the state for any particular patient) requires some kind of computer analysis...

By the time of our 1993 interviews, we found that specialized software had become available for such reporting. The finance director of the second nursing home in our sample informed us that

> both Medicaid and Medicare place restrictions...[that shape] the computing done here. First, Medicaid requires billing forms which are formatted so as to be acceptable to their system or they will not pay claims. Therefore, the software used here has to produce particular types of bills. Medicare requires a Patient Review Information (PRI) report—used to determine the necessity of various forms of treatment—and [another standardized report]—used to generate reimbursement for every patient it funds. It is now required that these be sent over Email in a form...compatible with the Medicare system.

Organizations like these nursing homes have no real alternative to accepting the computerized disciplines imposed in these ways. If the flow of information had remained as costly or time-consuming as it had been before the computer, they might have preserved a measure of insulation from state direction. But computing obviously makes it possible for the state to keep them on a short administrative leash. The finance director at [225] explained the fine-tuning of the computerized algorithms governing the compensation it receives from Medicaid:

> [T]his amount is determined as a combination of direct patient care (actual healthcare), indirect patient care (administrative) and a capital component. The greatest variable here is the direct patient care which is figured according to how sick the home's patients are. These reports are sent via modem to Medicaid...

These two nursing homes are extreme cases in our panel, in terms of the degree of regimentation of their affairs imposed via computerized linkage. We certainly would not portray them as more representative of the future of such arrangements than any number of other cases. Other such linkages range from such simple connections as direct access to account data held by a bank or accountant to sophisticated arrangements by which managers in one firm track the business of a newly-acquired subsidiary.

But it is clear that the new information technologies do open the way for a host of new kinds of relationships across organizational boundaries—providing all sorts of ways for organizations to "mind one another's business." Whether that involves imposing unequal power relations or reallocating tasks between co-equal partners, the potential for far-reaching qualitative change is apparent. Thus we believe that the role of computerized linkage between organizations deserves to be watched attentively. Should we revisit this or any other sample of typical organizations twenty years from now, we would expect to see still more striking and consequential arrangements of this kind.

Computing and the Rationalization of Work

The two nursing homes are unusual in that the terms of their computerization efforts were so largely dictated by a powerful outside agency. But many of the changes that they experienced in the wake of computerization are noteworthy for reasons quite unrelated to the power imbalance shaping their original adoption. The *rationalization* of the nursing homes' internal affairs triggered by computerization evidently had consequences that went well beyond their relations with the state of New York. We believe that the long-term processes of change launched by the applications discussed above, both in these and many other organizations, are highly consequential.

Typically such changes begin with the need, imposed by computerization, to "code" distinct elements of the organization's work— to assign different bits of activity to different categories, and to treat these bits differently. We see this pattern in the constraints described above in the case of [225]. Facing determined efforts by New York State to monitor virtually every aspect of its finances, that nursing home was required to provide a stream of data on matters ranging from the exact illnesses of, and care required by, each patient to time and expenses devoted to over-all management of the home. The net effect of these requirements was to trigger among management a degree of attention to the workings of the organization that would apparently not have existed, absent those requirements.

Though these "coding" processes were in effect imposed from outside, similar changes occur very widely on strictly internal initiatives. And once such coding becomes routine, the flow of work takes on a different aspect. The allocation of elements of work into analytical categories affords a new, more abstract view of the organization—and such views make it easy for decision-makers to spot further possibilities for rationalization.

In the other nursing home in our sample, the overview of the organization's work triggered by state-imposed computerization of work-flow had led to some notable innovations in selection of patients for admission. In the words of the interviewer,

...the new state requirements for billing and for determination of rates has led the home to get a computer for billing and now a PC for analyzing 'patient mixes.' A patient mix works like this: Say...that three nurses are being employed on the night shift for a ward of ten very ill or otherwise incapacitated patients. And say each of these patients can be billed at a rate of ten dollars per hour. What kinds of patients could replace any of these patients without losing revenue for the home?... Or to put it another way, what kinds of nursing resources are required for the kinds of ill patients (defined by the criteria that the state provides) to provide x amount of income for the home?

Thus, given broadened understanding of the cost and benefit implications of different "patient mixes," patients could now be admitted in terms of their potential profitability. By orchestrating just the right mix of illnesses and disabilities in its patient population, the home could maximize its profits. Note that this result was not part of anyone's intention when computerized billing requirements were imposed on this organization.

The point here is that the systematization engendered by computerization—whether imposed from the outside or inside—changes some basic constraints and possibilities for organizations. The schematic view of the organization emerging from computerized data reveals what might be called "deep structures" of workflow. New possibilities arise, new strategies become possible, in light of these altered visions. A further example from one of the nursing homes had to do with labor negotiations. Our informant, who had played a key role in computerizing the operations of the home, provided the following account:

The union lays out its requests (...for example, that employees be paid for all unused sick days). [The informant] is able to analyze the information he has by computer (i.e., how many sick days staff take, how much the home spends each year paying overtime to the employees who have to cover for absent workers). Using these calculations...management has a better grasp of what sorts of effects union demands will have in the long run, and...they can generate this information very quickly during bargaining sessions. This would not be possible if these sorts of calculations had to be done by hand.

Clearly labor relations issues had no role in the computerization that made these quick responses possible. But the fact that staffing information was now computerized shaped, at least potentially, the conduct of labor negotiations.

* * *

For nursing home managers, the key units of analysis are patients. But the pervasive effects of computerization on management mindsets seem to work in the same ways, whether the units are people or things. Another paradigmatic case from our panel involved not nursing home patients, but bottles of wine and spirits. Here we interviewed the young co-owner of a Manhattan neighborhood liquor store [114] who was gradually taking over its management from his parents. As he began his work in the shop, he found the existing computer system extremely inefficient and set about designing and implementing an improved system himself.

What he created was, in the classification we introduced in Chapter 3, a comprehensive system of inventory control and job tracking. Every bottle in the shop (whether on the display shelf or elsewhere in stock) was recorded in the computer memory. Computerized cash register point-of-sale devices automatically adjusted inventory for every sale, while automatically calculating price and tax and generating a sales slip. The computerized sales routine, according to our informant, made sales much quicker (a boon during busy times), while rendering mistakes over prices charged to customers practically impossible. Staff use of the cash register was monitored, so that any discrepancy between cash on hand and what sales should have yielded was easily spotted. The system automatically generated its own "need to order" reports when quantities of specific items in stock reached predetermined levels.

Though such systems are now widespread in small retail establishments, this one was rather futuristic in 1985, when our first interview with this establishment took place. What we find noteworthy here are the second- and third-order consequences of this application within the mindset of the owner-managers. According to our informant, it generated sales analyses affording easy comparison of sales of different categories of drink—or different brands, vendors, sizes of bottles, etc.—over periods of months or years. The result was a new overview of the business. In the words of our interviewer:

> First, you can spot trends. Certain liquors sell better in the summer. You can see HOW MUCH better they are selling and order smartly. When a vendor comes in and you want to order 13 cases and he says he'll give you a two percent discount if you order 20 cases, you run off a sales analysis and inventory sheet by vendor (it takes two minutes or less). Then, you can see if you should order more cases and if so which ones. E.g., "Well this vodka has been increasing the last four months by 10 bottles per month so I could take another case..." You may decide that the 2% discount isn't worth carrying the extra inventory. The sales analysis will show that if I order those extra 7 cases, I won't sell them for 3 months!

The interviewer described the system as providing

> more knowledge about the business. Where [the informant] is making money, and where he isn't. It has helped him make better decisions regarding inventory levels. He keeps the inventory leaner yet doesn't run out of anything.

Note that the information fueling this new, more analytical outlook was in some sense always "there," within the establishment. Indeed, the young man's parents (the previous managers of the shop) had made efforts to keep track of sales and inventory, by removing price tags from bottles upon sale and physically collecting them:

> Each night or the next morning the owner had to take out a book and write every item that was sold. The book was arranged by liquor and brand...and the owner kept all the inventory in these books. This took hours every week and still wasn't accurate...

* * *

We dwell on this case not because of anything extraordinary about it. On the contrary, except for the aggressive role of the young owner in designing and implementing these applications on his own, one finds parallels to these themes among the most heterogeneous variety of organizations in our sample.

At the other end of the size continuum, for example, [167], a giant suburban grocery chain, had computerized its inventory and ordering system for many of the same reasons that moved the young owner-manager of [114], and to much the same effect. There the sheer amount of inventory being controlled dwarfed the stock of the liquor store. At [167], individual store managers ordered by computer from a single remote warehouse. Still, the computer provided the same kind of advantage, by providing a more comprehensive and accurate overview of what was available, and by streamlining ordering from that stock.

And here, too, the fact that the computerized system monitored goods in real time provided significant advantages in terms of reordering. In this case, the use of point-of-sale scanners provided an additional source of information to buyers, beyond what they could learn from the computerized inventory itself. At the time of our first interviews, these devices were in use in only some of the stores comprising the chain. As our interviewer noted,

> From the stores with optical scanning equipment they get a stock movement report which is even more timely...and more valuable because it shows what is actually

> SELLING. [By contrast], the warehouse stock report is one step removed from the sale. It tells you what the store managers order for their stores, but it doesn't tell you whether the item is sold or not. This is important, for example if you want to gauge the success of a sale. With the scanning equipment, you know immediately if a sale is successful. With the warehouse report you only know that store managers are ordering more...and not whether [the items ordered] are actually selling.

By tracking sales in real time, then, this system provides bases for more precise, better-informed buying decisions.

Many of these same dynamics were also salient in another large establishment—a nationally known marketer of men's clothing. At the time of our first contact with this company in 1985, [37] employed some 750 staff in a variety of locations. Our interviewer gave the following account of the constraints of business in this company, as related by the vice president he interviewed:

> One of the key facts of life for this company is that its product specifications change from season to season... [Thus] timing is everything...timing in getting raw material for the planned fashion line for the season coming up, timing in getting the material from place to place in a very complex system of production, timing in getting it into the warehouse and then shipped out at a precise moment... Their contracts with their customers stipulate that their product will arrive on a specific date—if the product is late in arriving, the sale is automatically off... [S]elling in the volatile world of luxury fashion goes by the week... One day late can be a disaster. [37] has sold 11 million dollars worth of shirts, for example, in a single day.

Hence the pressing need for precise and timely information on what is available to be sold, and when. Here computing was reported to have made a considerable difference:

> [T]he main problem with selling from the old days was...overselling—that is, selling a certain item from a certain line and then discovering that there were none left... [The computerized] system basically allows salesmen to know within 24 hours if there is available stock so that he might sell a different item from available stock or write a back order... This sales tool has saved the company some 8 million dollars which otherwise would have been lost, since salesmen before did not have the knowledge needed to go back to a customer and sell a different item or write a back order until it was too late.

Note the parallels between these uses of computing and the sophisticated system for managing the activity of buyers reported by the well-known Manhattan clothing retailer discussed in Chapter 4. That system, by extremely close monitoring of sales on the shop floor, "knew" exactly how well the products selected by each of the store's buyers was doing at every point in time. Based on this knowledge, management either extended or restricted the budget available to each buyer from day to day, if not from hour to hour.

This same ability of computer systems to keep track in real time of countless discrete elements of work—from nursing home patients and their specific disabilities to colors favored by consumers of men's shirts—and thereby to husband scarce resources presents itself in the greatest variety of contexts. Further examples were reported by a large Manhattan law firm. This organization employed about 340 at the time of our first interview, roughly half of them lawyers. Here the critical commodity was neither nursing home patients and their maladies nor any form of inanimate merchandise, but high-priced lawyers' time.

The firm had adopted several applications for managing that crucial resource. One was a program that produced itemized bills—something of an innovation in itself in this profession—taking account of different rates billed by more and less senior lawyers. Another was a "docket scheduling system" that monitored such things as dates for court appearances, briefs filed, motions made, etc. for each attorney at the firm. Both these applications were reported to provide a more comprehensive and detailed view to top management of how each lawyer was using his or her time.

A third application took these trends a step farther. This they called their "case management data base," which summarized resources devoted by the firm to each of its pending cases. Our interviewer described it as including

> basic information such as parties in the case, date of court activities, location, lawyers involved [on both sides], reporting requirements [to the firm's clients]... A dollar value is assigned to each case...

Like the inventory control systems discussed above, or the system guiding the budget discretion for [247] buyers, this one forms the basis for some critical and distinctive decision-making:

> Management...can make judgements as to where to put emphasis. Do we have enough lawyers working on this five million dollar case? Do we think they're the right lawyers for the case?

A final example comes from a Manhattan-based printing company, [238]. Readers may recall the discussion in Chapter 3 of applications adopted at this establishment; these included a job-tracking system that had the apparently serendipitous effect of drawing attention to highly-paid printers' failure to notify management when presses broke down. A subsequently adopted application in this establishment organized data on rates it paid to newspapers and other media for carrying the ads that it produced. These placement costs represented a major expense and required scanning of advertising rates and circulation data to identify the most cost-effective carriers. Managers accordingly assigned two staff to creating and maintaining a comprehensive database on these matters. Thus, in the words of our interviewer, if

> the firm knows that if it does 12 insertions during the year in [a Baltimore newspaper] rather than 11, they will get a much better rate per insertion...the sales force will spend time getting together clients for...[additional ads]...
>
> It is an easy calculation...to figure the rate per person that the ad will reach. If a particular paper seems very high, they won't advertise as much there.

The partner we interviewed claimed that this application had saved the company fifty thousand dollars the previous year. Asked how the same purposes were accomplished before computerization, he noted that these activities were

> never done systematically. Some [staff]...were aware of some of these figures and some of these rate structures, but as the firm grew from dealing with a few markets and maybe 100 papers to dealing with many markets and 500 papers, no one could keep up with this information.

Like many companies in this sample, [238] here found itself using its recently acquired computing resources in ways not originally anticipated—to deal with business problems that may not have been clearly conceptualized when the applications involved were adopted.

* * *

We could furnish examples like these from virtually every sector of our sample. Notwithstanding the variety of different forms taken by computing, certain commonalities stand out in the role of computerized work in the mindsets of decision-makers. Specifically,

1. Computing encourages, and often compels decision-makers to *disaggregate* work into its constituent elements, and to *code* these elements in the course of recording them in the computer. This coding operation obviously requires development of some form of comprehensive category scheme.

2. Such coding, when carried out systematically, yields *summary, analytical overviews* of organizational processes.

3.   These overviews prod managers to *identify trends* and to *distinguish notable risks and opportunities*—and to use such knowledge as bases for strategic decision-making. The result is to render areas of organizational life that previously remained matters of guesswork and happenstance subject to control and planning.

4.   Concomitantly, computing makes it possible to monitor complex processes as they unfold, leading to more *highly discriminating, real-time action* to profit from fleeting opportunities or avoid abrupt losses.

Conclusion

The vision of revolution in management as fueled by the computer has inspired many imaginative prophecies of organizational transformation. From new access to information, it is held, come new ways of understanding the essential nature of work. And these new ways of understanding are surely bound to foster new management practices and structures.

Certainly many individual scenarios from our sample support such expectations. In aggregate, however, the cases in this sample show relatively few of the structural changes most often envisaged by commentators. We find no evidence that management hierarchies are growing systematically more hierarchical or more democratic in the course of computerization, for example. We do find that high rates of computerization among our panel cases tend to reduce the proportion of staff made up of clerical workers, but not that of management. Yet analysis of case studies also reminds us that "the same" technologies can be associated with very different "effects" within specific organizations.

We also find evidence that computing is making possible new forms of inter-organizational linkage—some of which appear to alter the agendas and repertoires of the organizations involved. Though the cases turned up in this sample represent no more than straws in the wind, we believe that the rise of such linkages bears attention as the ability of organizations to exploit these technologies unfolds.

And finally, we find a still more pervasive and intriguing tendency of computing to induce more systematic ways of thinking about organizational processes among those who direct the organizations. These amount to a spur to classic, Weberian *rationalization*—with all sorts of far-reaching consequences for performance of organizations and their role in their larger social contexts.

Appendix 6.1

Proportion of Staff Allocated to Various Job Categories 1985 and 1993 (N=81)[a].

Job Categories	1985 Panel Establishments		1993 Panel Establishments		Change in Proportion of Staff 1985-1993	
	Mean	SD	Mean	SD	Mean	SD
Proportion of Total Staff	*100.0*	-	*100.0*	-		
Management	11.0	10.0	12.4	10.4	1.4	6.3
Professional	9.3	19.9	8.3	17.9	-0.9	7.0
Sales	7.8	15.3	10.1	18.5	2.4	12.0
Clerical	23.3	22.6	20.0	22.1	-3.3	11.3
Shop Floor/Warehouse	43.7	36.8	40.4	35.3	-3.3	10.8
Maintenance/Janitorial	2.0	8.9	2.6	9.3	0.6	4.6
Programmers/Computing	0.5	1.8	0.7	2.0	0.2	1.3
Other	2.5	13.7	5.4	16.0	2.9	9.2

SD: Standard Deviation

[a]One organization missing due to missing responses for job categories.

7

Conclusions

A pervasive tension has shaped virtually all of this book: the tension between the mythology of computerization, and experience in the ordinary computerizing organizations of our sample.

Even in the most mundane settings, the role of that mythology was abundantly apparent. Decision-makers, we found, were willing to adopt computer applications whose actual effects could scarcely be known in advance, on a diffuse grant of credibility extended to the "revolutionary" potentials of the technology. Such credibility apparently lost little force, even in the face of direct experience—witness the rarity with which computer applications were *dropped* during the period covered in our study. The usefulness of computing to organizations is difficult to assess, even for those closest at hand. In the absence of certainty on such matters, decision-makers draw on a ready store of received understandings. Any effort to document and analyze the actual unfolding of computerization must focus on the interaction between such mythic images and the constraints and directions experienced by those seeking to deal with the technology. And such efforts raise their own questions of interpretation.

Two Ways of Understanding and Misunderstanding Computerization

Two sharply contrasting mindsets have shaped scholarly research on computing in organizations.

The first of these we might call the "theoretical" approach—in the loose sense by which that term is applied to ideas derived from the classic sociological tradition of Saint Simon, Marx, or Adam Smith. Distinctive of this approach is the elaboration of a model of a single, master social process seen as describing a broad range of social change. Examples might include Saint Simon's vision of scientific and technological thinking as the engine for infusing rationality in all phases of social practice; or Adam Smith's image of the dulling of worker sensitivities through participation in mass production, even as productivity flourished; or Marx's model of the erosion of the autonomy of the artisan, as more and more of production comes under the sway of profit-seeking capitalists.

Much contemporary writing on computerization, and countless other subjects, follows this mode. That is, it seeks to identify a key process of transformation—perhaps a single cause-effect chain—that underlies and gives coherence to otherwise disparate patterns of social and technological change. Thus, for example, we have Zuboff's vivid characterization of the tension between possibilities for enrichment of work through "informatization" versus the dangers of imposition of unilateral power via computerization; or Drucker's vision of computerization as fostering more collegial, information-based management structures; or Braverman's grim model of automation (including computerization) as a master opportunity for management to squeeze skill and discretion from everyday work.

The images generated by "theoretical" thinking in this sense are often incandescent. Some are so powerful as to short-circuit our thinking from other processes that may deserve no less analytical attention. No one who takes the trouble to understand Marx's interpretation of the expropriation of artisans by technologies set in place by capital is apt to forget it. Since Marx, many of his followers have amplified that image with variations like that of Harry Braverman. Other classic theorists of technology and social change, from Adam Smith to Thorstein Veblen, continue similarly to supply inspirational master-images for present-day understandings.

The trouble with these inspirations is that the dramatic impact of the image involved may tell us rather little about the frequency with which the process in question applies—or about its importance relative to other, possibly quite different processes. We have registered skepticism on these grounds concerning nearly all the encompassing theoretical models encountered in this study. Theoretical social science is good at generating what one author has called "sometimes true" representations of our subject matter; our problem, in this research and elsewhere, is to discern just how widely they hold.

Quite the opposite approach is adopted by another group of analysts—one is tempted to call this the "a-theoretical" school. We refer here to the widespread quest for computer "effects" through correlational analyses of large data sets. If the term "a-theoretical" is deserved, it is where such studies slight attention to the detail of the specific organizational processes by which the "effects" in question are produced. In this book, we have most often encountered this thinking as applied to the "effects" of computing on productivity and employment. But the same approach can be discerned in statistical quests for "effects" on communication patterns, management hierarchy, or any number of other variables.

The knowledge emanating from such studies certainly has its own value. There are all sorts of good reasons for wanting to know, for example, whether computerizing organizations are more likely than others to add or shed employees at any particular point. But problems of interpretation arise when one seeks to draw the implications of such knowledge for new settings—including the "same" settings at later points in time.

By failure to attend to specific social mechanisms by which change in computing leads, or fails to lead, to the hypothesized "effect," investigators may be led astray. If "effects" are registered, some may conclude that they represent a-contextual facts of life—like the relationships between temperature, pressure, and volume of gasses, or between time and the decay of radioactive elements. In social inquiry, one can expect few such robust relationships. In the case of computerization, we have sought to emphasize, "the same" technologies may readily lead to quite different "effects," as contexts vary. One must beware of the possibility that the quantitative "effects" of computerization may in fact reflect a mix of quite different specific processes—a mix subject to change in different settings at the same time, or in the "same" settings over time.

Issues of this kind are of course hardly restricted to analyses of technology. In a work entitled *Social Mechanisms*, a number of authors have recently decried the results of failure to grasp the diversity of social processes underlying a wide variety of social "effects," for example,

A statistical association between "class" and income, or "class" and health, tells us that individuals from certain "classes" have lower incomes or worse health than others, but it says nothing about why this is the case. To answer such questions, it is necessary to introduce and explicate the generative mechanisms that might have produced the ob-

served differences in average income or health between the occupational groups that the
researchers have assigned to different "classes." A statistical "effect" of a class variable in
contexts like these is essentially an indicator of our inability to specify properly the
underlying explanatory mechanisms. (Hedstrom and Swedberg 1998, p. 11)

We imagine that authors pursuing the "effects" of computing on
productivity or related variables *do*, in fact, have one rather general
mechanism in mind—a mechanism involving efficient substitution
of computing for human labor, or for other more expensive business costs. We have illustrated, in Chapter 5 and elsewhere, how
such processes occur among the organizations in our sample. But
we have also sought to portray a variety of other mechanisms and
processes in which incorporation of computing to an organization's
repertoire of activities may lead to no such "effects"—though it may
nevertheless trigger all sorts of other noteworthy changes.

In short, we see two broad dangers in the single-minded pursuit
of computing "effects" through aggregate statistical analysis. On
one hand, such efforts may lead analysts to overlook important
mechanisms where they in fact exist—for example, in cases where
different processes simply cancel one another statistically. Here conclusions of "no effect" may in fact conceal underlying realities of
great richness. We would not expect medical researchers to interpret a rise in rates of Hepatitis-A in conjunction with a commensurate decline in Hepatitis-B as "no change" in the prevalence of hepa-
titis, after all. It is no more than prudent to adopt the same attitude
toward our subject matter here.

The second hazard is that discovery of statistical "effects" may
lead us to imagine that we know more than we really do about how
the association in question comes about—that is, about which specific mechanisms are responsible for such results. Thus, the work
that we report here leads us to suspect that computerization reduces
net employment in establishments in many cases, increases it in
others, and leaves it quantitatively unaffected elsewhere. Under these
circumstances, the greatest interest ought to attach, not to the existence of the "effect" in any one body of data, but to the mix of
mechanisms likely to produce outcomes of interest in subsequent
investigations.

* * *

We conclude that both these mindsets—the "theoretical" fixation
on salient social processes and the quest for aggregate "effects" that

may distract attention from the specifics of *any* such processes—present characteristic virtues and pitfalls. An optimal strategy for understanding the social role of computerization would combine elements of the two approaches. It would begin by seeking to create what one might call a *library* of qualitatively distinct social processes—well-documented mechanisms by which computerization interacts with human intent, social structure, staffing requirements, productivity dynamics, and other variables of evident analytical interest. Such a "library" would make it possible to assess the rates of occurrence of such processes within specific bodies of data. These assessments might lead in turn to quantitative analyses aiming at explaining change in aggregate results across populations—and at predicting such changes under specific future conditions.

Such predictions, under this optimal scenario, would not simply have to rely on the assumption that the future will most likely resemble the past. If one could know how the "mix" of constituent social processes were changing within any population of interest, one would have grounds to predict how changing conditions might lead to changes in aggregate "effects."

Few domains of social science inquiry actually attract the concerted efforts necessary to produce such satisfying results. In this study, we can at best hope to nudge existing scholarly debate in this direction. We have sought to develop, in our analyses of specific cases, models of discrete mechanisms by which computing becomes incorporated into the workings of organizations. We have sought to show how "the same" technologies, applied to "the same sorts of organizations" can yield quite different "effects." And we have tried to demonstrate how the models of such incorporation that have won widest attention can rarely, if ever, describe the full range of possibilities.

Let us review a few salient conclusions from these efforts.

The Computer "Revolution"

If one term has seen more than its share of use in discussion of the social role of computing, it is surely "revolution." Few commentators have been able to resist characterizing the technology as "revolutionary"—though closer attention to their words makes it plain that they have many different sorts of revolutions in mind.

Viewed from our sample of typical New York organizations, the initial adoption of computing appears decidedly *un*revolutionary. True, the decision-makers we interviewed often seemed willing to ascribe the most far-reaching powers to information technologies *in general*. But the actual process of instating new computer operations, as reported in these rank-and-file establishments, proceeded in piecemeal, ad-hoc, decidedly unrevolutionary steps. Computerization programs that transform the structures of organization or the content of work relationships from top to bottom are nowhere to be found in this sample.

Instead, computing takes root in the form of discrete additions to established work routines, mostly by substituting computer applications for specific conventional operations, from payroll to accounts payable, to inventory-maintenance. These steps are not taken with the intent of creating drastic qualitative change in the workplace, but as means for resolving specific management problems: bottlenecks in workflow, uncontrolled costs, failures in coordination across elements of the organization, etc.

Newly adopted computing applications, by the same token, overwhelmingly serve standard business purposes, rather than particularly "high-tech," futuristic practices. In this sample, four such purposes characterized the great majority of all applications: financial accounting; inventory control; job tracking; and word processing. Note that these are generic activities that one might well encounter in nearly any organization. Computing is rarely if ever adopted *in the first instance* to support qualitatively new activities in organizations, activities that were not being carried out before, or could not be accomplished *at all* in its absence.

Nor have we encountered much evidence that computing activities are adopted in a highly predictable order. Accounting applications were adopted in great numbers throughout the period covered by the study, whereas order entry applications were more likely to be instated at the beginning and word processing was more likely to be adopted at the end of the period. But we find nothing like a "natural history" of computing adoption, in which one form of computing activity must necessarily be in place before others can appear.

Cost-Effectiveness and Employment

One of the most basic and widespread expectations governing computing adoption is, of course, that it represents a rational investment of scarce economic resources. Perhaps for this reason, some of the most widely noted scholarly debates on computing have focused on the attempts to demonstrate such cost-effectiveness across large populations of organizations.

Accordingly, we have looked carefully for evidence that computerization in our organizations between 1985 and 1993 might enhance their cost-effectiveness. The case studies provided mixed evidence on this score. Some establishments provided accounts of computing applications that, from all the facts made available to us, appeared highly cost-effective, in comparison to the conventional routines that they replaced. The adoption of other applications, by contrast, often made it appear extremely speculative as to whether any such effects would be measurable. Often, computing adoption seemed to reflect that diffuse grant of credibility accorded to it by the mythology surrounding the technology.

In the quest for *aggregate* evidence of cost-effectiveness across the organizations in our panel, our analyses showed little evidence that computerization enhanced cost-effectiveness in any way that we could measure. Computerization seemed to have no bearing on the likelihood of an organization's going out of business, for example. Further, a series of multivariate analyses showed no strong relationship between rates of computerization in our panel cases and change in the proxy variable for efficiency.

Another major focus of public and scholarly attention has been the role of computerization in changing employment levels. Most economists, and many managers in our sample, have seen the technology above all as a substitute for human labor. Our panel data, however, show a net tendency for computerization to be followed by *increased* staffing levels. Here, too, the site interviews also documented specific instances where results of computerization took the opposite direction—sometimes resulting in forestalled hiring or redeployment of staff, sometimes causing outright job losses. Other site interviews, unsurprisingly, illustrated quite the opposite sorts of "effects."

Note that these findings, even to the extent that they generalize to other organizations, leave open certain important questions of aggregate "effects." The very ability of organizations like those in this study to shed staff in the course of computerization may presuppose growth in employment in other organizations elsewhere in the economy. Companies that eliminate secretarial staff by requiring salespersons and managers to do their own word processing, for instance, are in effect relying on organizations elsewhere to create

and maintain word processing software. Judging whether staff reductions in rapidly computerizing organizations like those in our
sample are balanced by growth elsewhere in the "information
economy" is beyond the scope of a study like this.

Management Forms and Supervision of Work

For many authors, the salient promise of computing in organizations has been to change basic patterns of management. Some of
these prophecies have been optimistic, foreseeing the rise of less
hierarchical, more collegial management styles. Others have imag-
ined a world in which computerization renders management supervision more minute and oppressive. In the latter case, a common
vision has computerization creating a comprehensive and unfor-
giving record of every moment of every worker's day. Both the
positive and negative visions have been combined with predictions
of profound structural changes in the workplace—ranging from
categorical reduction in basic categories of workers to abrupt sharp-
ening or flattening of management hierarchies.

Statistics from our sample give no evidence of *net* changes attributable to computing in sharpness of management hierarchies. In
this respect, rapidly computerizing organizations were no more likely
than others to grow flatter or steeper in their shape.

With respect to distributions of staff across job categories, the
story is a bit more complex. In individual cases, we documented a
number of instances where specific computerization efforts resulted
in dramatic gains or losses to specific job categories—to the extent
of complete elimination of clerical staff as a direct result of computerization in at least one case. In aggregate analyses, proportions of
establishment staff engaged in clerical work showed clear reduction attributable to computerization between the two data points in
our study—even as high rates of computerization resulted in net
gains to total staff. Higher levels of computerization in 1985 were
also associated with reduced levels of clerical staffing in 1993. No
such differences could be associated with any other job category.

Nor did the case studies provide much support for ideas that computing would bring comprehensive changes in the nature of work
supervision. Only one organization had adopted anything like the
comprehensive surveillance throughout an entire workplace envisaged in the worst-case scenarios from the literature. True, computing often serves to monitor work performance both collectively and

individually—particularly via sales analyses. But such monitoring overwhelmingly took the form of collection of relatively discrete bits of information, at specific (and expectable) points in job performance.

Our inquiries left us equally skeptical of notions that computerization necessarily leads to loss in the autonomy or quality of work experience. True, few of our interviews gave us the chance to focus at length on workers' reactions to the technology. But in that minority of cases where we could form an impression of the actual experience of work, computerization did not necessarily appear as a villain. Some computerized work routines seem to have automated the less interesting aspects of jobs; even some forms of work monitoring seemed to be welcomed by workers for providing evidence of good job performance. Here, as elsewhere, it appears that the auspices of computerization—above all, the intents of those who put it into practice—are vastly more important than any fundamental characteristics of the technology in shaping its "effects."

Finally, we note some tentative evidence that computing may be fostering new management structures *across* organizational boundaries. The close interactive coordination afforded by computing makes it possible for organizations to "mind one another's business" in ways that would otherwise be impossible. The net effect can be to change the division of labor between or among organizational partners. One manifestation of such change is the ability of the more powerful organizations to micro-manage the affairs of their less powerful partners. Another—sometimes tantamount to the same thing—may be the rise of "strategic information systems," in which aggressive organizations reshape the choices available to their organizational partners, or to the customers of the latter.

Computing as a Self-Justifying Enterprise

Diametrically opposed to standard economic and sociological thinking on computing is the Ellulian vision of technological change as self-justifying process. Instead of an instrumental step to reduce objective "problems," Ellul and his followers hold that technological innovation represents a response to needs created by the technological mindset. Though deeply counter-intuitive to most observers, this model is not without support among our cases. Clearly computing can and does create new "needs"—needs satisfied by itself. Once word processing became widespread, for example, "needs" for highly presentable letters, memos, tables, and the like seemed to grow in proportion to the ability of the technology to fulfill them. And at least one of our interviewees mentioned that computerized estimates to prospective clients appeared, to him, to command better attention than handwritten versions. Another informant expressed the view that bills produced by computer seemed to get paid more readily than old-fashioned bills.

Decisions about adoption of computing applications documented in this research, we have argued, are often highly conjectural. In many cases, managers have operated under considerable uncertainty as to the actual costs and benefits likely to result from their decisions. In such conditions, diffuse perceptions of "needs" for computerization may have far-reaching consequences. The resulting demand for computers and related products could well help stimulate the economy, without necessarily making much difference in the productivity of organizations acquiring them.

These and other findings from the study should spur reflection about judgments of the productivity of computerization in the aggregate, as well as within single organizations. Part of the definition of productivity, of course, involves what decision-makers are willing to pay for—and the mythology of computing clearly has a vast bearing on such willingness. A fascinating series of economic analyses showed a productivity surge in the computer industry in the United States at the end of 1999. The cause, apparently, was a surge in purchases of equipment and services aimed at warding off the threatened "Y2K" debacle, in which computing systems were expected to be disabled by their inability to distinguish between the year 2000 and any other year ending with "00." In retrospect, there seems reason to believe that those dangers were considerably exaggerated—either through sincere excess of prudence or by design. To the extent that that "need" for computing indeed responded to some form of mythology, what do we make of the productivity gains of the organizations that rose to meet the need? This is a question that tests the limits of some crucial analytical concepts.

Computing and the Rationalization of Work

Throughout this work, as we have sought to specify what changes are triggered by computing in organizations, we have found ourselves responding in effect, "It all depends..." Context, we have insisted, always matters enormously. Whether computing enriches work or deprives it of all fulfillment; whether it generates new employment or reduces staffing; whether it makes workplaces more hierarchical or more collegial—for all these important questions we see the characteristics of the setting of computerization as more important than the content of the technology itself. Thus the quest for distinctive "effects" of computing may become a burden or a distraction from recognizing the forces or circumstances that matter most.

But if this were our only response to the question of what difference computing makes, we would be flying in the face of most classic views of technology and social change. One of the distinctive guiding inspirations for sociologists of technology has always been that the *aims* and *intents* guiding the introduction of technologies do not tell the full story of their *results*. The tools we use, in other words, impose new mindsets, or alter balances of power, or create unexpected new relationships, or legitimate new categories of activity—or bring about any number of results that may have been no part of the intentions of those who set the changes in motion. The guiding aim of the sociological study of technology, in this view, ought to be generalizations about the character of these unintended transformations.

What generalizations does this study have to offer, then? Obviously, any response has to be cast in highly abstract terms, if it is to apply to the full range of organizations and settings considered here. But we have pinpointed certain forms of change that seem to hold very widely. Salient among these is the pervasive role of computing in *rationalizing* organizational action along the lines described at the end of the last chapter.

A widespread result of computerization, we are convinced, is the transformation of decision-makers' *vision* of their organizations. In its most diverse forms, computing nudges decision-makers to classify the work of their organizations into conceptually distinct categories—identifying and distinguishing among processes and conditions that might otherwise go unnoticed in the absence of the technology. The computer-driven inclination to grasp such hitherto latent patterns, and concomitant opportunities to respond to them in real time, create potentials for organizations to perform in ways that may have been no part of anyone's intention at the time of the decision to computerize.

In some ways these "effects" of computerization may seem to parallel those envisaged by Saint Simon and his latter-day disciple,

Daniel Bell. Recall the passage from Bell's *The Coming of Post-Modern Society* that we quoted in Chapter 1, where he describes computing as serving to help "master 'scale'"—by which he seems to mean very complex and far-reaching processes like those involved in management of large public and private organizations (1973, p. 42). Such mastery is achieved, he argues, through the application of *scientific* or *theoretical* thinking to the administration of human affairs.

But the role of science or theory as envisaged by Bell is not exactly what we mean by the rationalizing force of computing. True, the applications of the technology documented from our sample do mobilize the sorts of orderly thinking supposedly essential to science—as well as to business, public administration, orchestral music, and a host of other activities governed by classic Weberian rationality. But the computerized activities that we have encountered only rarely involve scientific principles or processes narrowly speaking.

What they *do* encourage is a more effective, systematic pursuit of the means-ends calculations that are standard in businesses and other formal organizations. They nudge decision-makers to identify patterns, commonalities, and trends in their work—and thereby open the way to extend purposeful decision-making to domains of organizational life that would otherwise be left to guesswork and happenstance. Whether computerization involves accounting, job-tracking, inventory, or even simply word processing, the result is to bring new, more abstract forms of information to light and thereby—sooner or later—present decision-makers with new options. The sheer *speed* of response afforded by computing often makes it possible to exercise these options in real time. The targets of such rationalization vary, in our sample, from the mix of patients in nursing homes, to the stocking of bottles in liquor stores, to warehouse inventories in supermarket chains, to budgets extended to buyers in a stylish New York clothier, to the allocation of high-priced lawyers' time. But underlying our highly diverse cases, parallels in the thought-ways engendered by the technology are unmistakable.

We scarcely argue that these trends are equally consequential for all organizations or in all applications from our study. Some computing applications indeed seem to alter about as much of the mentality of those who use them as an electric toaster might do in the thoughts of the householders who use it to prepare their breakfast.

But we do see few, if any, authentic *counterexamples*, cases where computing actually *narrows* decision-makers' vision of their work or *reduces* the level of abstraction in their thinking.

On the other hand, the rationalizing incentives of computing come in extremely diverse and unexpected ways. Even off-the-shelf word processing applications have the potential to generate data on numbers of words typed or length of sentences, or to enable users to entertain different formats for presentation of their work. Over all, we judge, computing tends to generate for its users access to widened ranges of possibilities—and hence, ultimately, to a broadened scope for rationalizing trends that have long been fundamental in the evolution of formal organizations.

Conclusion

We propose a view of computerization at the organizational grass roots level considerably less dramatic than that detailed in the mythology of computing—yet one which by no means minimizes the potentials of the technology. If this study is any guide, the role of computing in American organizations will mostly prove incremental and will accelerate slowly. Most organizations will continue to adopt computing, most of the time, to resolve delimited, concrete management problems. Organizations whose workings are transformed from top to bottom by radically new computerized techniques will remain a minority phenomenon. But in the long run, we expect that the trends described above will increase the grip of decision-makers on their organizations, rendering them more efficient and more innovative in a host of ways.

None of this gives reason to believe that these rationalizing patterns will of themselves increase the *wisdom* of management policy or enhance the values of a humane or mind-expanding workplace. The sort of rationality we identify here is strictly formal or instrumental. It leaves untouched the ultimate ends to which efficient means are applied. Whether the organizational world being created by the changes considered here will be a better one to inhabit is not a question whose answer can be sought in the nature of technology.

Appendix 7.1

Sample of Complete 1985 Interview

Firm:

Interview with:

Date:

Part I

1. What does this company make or do?

    a. Approximately how many customers do you have? Approximately how many invoices do you process per month?

2. When was this company founded?

    a. Is it private _____ or public? _____

3. Is this the only location of the firm?

        Yes _____ No _____

    a. If no, where are the other locations?

    b. Is this the headquarters _____, a subsidiary _____, division _____, branch _____, franchise _____, other _____, of a larger company?

4. How many people work in this company now?

    _____ management (upper and middle, not immediate supervisors) Professionals

    _____ Sales/Marketing

    _____ Clerical-Financial-Records

    _____ Production-Shop Floor-Stockeeping-Wharehouse

    _____ Maintenance-Janitorial-I

    _____ Full-time programmers-Systems analysts-Operators

    _____ Craft and Technicians

    _____ Other (describe)

Are any workers unionized?

If this is headquarters, how many work for company as a whole?

    a. How many levels of management are there in this firm? (include boss and supervisor)?

    b. Has this changed since computing?

5. What computers does this company use?

(Machine When Purchased, Micro? Mini? mainframe?, Total # standalones? Total # terminals?)

total number of terminals: stand-alone computers:

total number of computerized machines:

total number of dedicated word processors:

6. Are these your first computers?

      Yes _____ No _____

      a. If not, when did you computerize and what happened?

      b. When you first computerized, what did you want the machine to do?

7.   What applications do you use these computers for? In what order did these come?
     What business activities are computerized in your firm? (Please check off those
     applications that are computerized)

Financial

_____ Accounts Payable and Receivable

_____ Invoices and Billing

_____ General Ledger

_____ Financial Statements (Balance Sheet, P&L, Cash Flow)

_____ Financial Forecasting or Modeling (e.g. Spreadsheets) Taxes and tax returns

_____ Investments

_____ Fixed Assets

_____ Depreciation

_____ Cost accounting or cost control

_____ Payroll

Orders, Sales and Purchasing

_____ Order Entry

_____ Job costing, pricing or estimating Customer Service

_____ Checking customer's credit

_____ Purchase order processing

_____ Sales analysis or marketing analysis

_____ Commissions on sales

_____ Shipping and receiving

_____ Inventory Control (finished goods only)

_____ Point of Sales (computerized cash registers)

Manufacturing

_____ Computer Aided Design (CAD)

_____ Bill of Materials

_____ Job scheduling or tracking

_____ MRP

_____ Work measurement systems (output of machine operators)

_____ Measurement of machine downtime

_____ Numerically controlled machine tools (N/Cg CNC, DNC)

_____ Computerized Testing Equipment

_____ Scrap Measurement

Paperwork

_____ Word Processing (LIMITED)

_____ Mailing Lists and labels

_____ Records and filing

_____ Graphics, charts, etc.

_____ Typesetting

_____ Scheduling Appointments

_____ Personnel records and reports (Human Resources)

_____ Tracking paperwork

_____ Work measurement systems (output of clerical workers)

Other

_____ Networking/communications with other computers

_____ Education, training

_____ Scientific, Engineering, or R&D

Please tell us if you have any other computer applications not listed here.

a. All in house _____ Any outside services _____

8. What was the total staff at this establishment when the first of these computers was introduced?

9. What were the approximate revenues of the firm the year computing was first introduced?

10. What were the approximate annual revenues of the firm this last year?

11. Other than computing have there been any particularly notable changes in this establishment in the past few years?

Part II

Firm:

Application #:

Identify Application:

1. What exactly does this application do?

2. How long has this application been up and in use?

3. What categories of staff, and how many of each work directly with the computer? (specify)

4. What other people use the system?
   a. How does the system alter the work roles of those involved with it? (pace, interest, duties, skill, supervision, saves time/people do other things)

5. What kinds of decisions depend on its use?

6. Where does the raw data for this application come from?

7. What does this application enable the company to know or do that could not be known or done otherwise?
   b. Do you keep closer track of staff?
   c. What new patterns of interaction are allowed, or what new ones are broken? (are people more isolated or do they interact more)

8. Have the number of people employed changed through the use of this application? (provide numbers) Are these the same people as in any other application?

   Shrunk _____

   Shrunk, less work _____

   Shrunk, more work _____

   No change _____

   No change, more work _____

   Increased _____

   Increased, more work _____
   a. Kinds of workers changed?
   b. If you had to do the work you now do without computers how many people would have to be employed? (is the work qualitatively different? could the work be done at all manually?)

9. How satisfied are employees with this application?

10. Was there substantial turnover? Was it because of computers?

11. How satisfied does management claim to be with the system? (advantages, disadvantages)

12. How often does the system go down?

        Daily _____

        weekly _____

        Monthly _____

        Less frequently _____

        Never _____

13. What happens when the system goes down? backup system?

14. What was the introduction of this application like (technical, staff problems? Did it take time to change work routines?)

15. Any problems since the introduction? (technical or staff?)

16. How were the purposes served by this application accomplished before it went up? (Activity done manually; how? Activity qualitatively new to the firm?)

17. What sort of thinking led decision-makers to adopt this application?

_____ bottleneck; response to problem

_____ heard about it from customers, suppliers?

_____ read about it somewhere? where?

_____ key decision-maker was a technology enthusiast decision compelled by competitive pressure?

Was a formal cost-benefit analysis done?

18. Does the original decision appear to have made sense in light of experience? (have the original reasons to adopt computing been borne out by experience?)

19. Has the existence of the computing capability in this application led to a search for new ways of using this capability? (explain? Has search been successful?)

20. How, if at all, has this application changed relations between the firm and its customers, suppliers or others outside the firm?

Part III

1. Has the adoption of computing changed the way this company as a whole is managed?

2. How have computers changed your job and the job of other managers?

a. availability, accuracy and timeliness of data

b. easier to pin down responsibility for problems no change

c. clearer channels of authority no change

d. better control and monitoring of subordinates no change

e. increased ability to plan ahead slightly

f. increased speed of organizational response

g. greater/less discretion/autonomy in your own work

h. increase/decrease delegation of decisions to others

i. shift in how manager allocates his time and performs his duties

2b. Are there ways in which being computerized makes your job or the job of other managers more difficult?

3. If you look back on your experiences with computer technology, how would you rate them?

   Very satisfied _____

   Somewhat satisfied _____

   Neutral _____

   Somewhat dissatisfied _____

   Very dissatisfied _____

4. What are your future plans?

Appendix 7.2

Sample of Complete 1993 Interview

Firm: _____

Interviewee _____

Initial Interviewee _____

Telephone _____

Date _____

Old Case Number _____

Information from old interviews to be inserted in bracketed spaces: [   ].

101 Begin interview: "Now I see that you participated in our earlier study in [month, year]. Could I ask whether, since that time, [this establishment] has undergone any especially dramatic or noteworthy changes?"

If respondent seems unsure how to interpret the question: "For example, have there been any unusual changes in management, sales volume, the products or services you provide, or anything like that?"

If yes, record discursive response

102 "In our last interview, you were described as [ ]. Is this description still accurate?"

If not, specify

103 "In our last interview, this was described as [the sole location/a branch/the headquarters, etc.] of [this establishment]. Is this still the case?"

If no, record new status

104 "What is the total number of employees now working at [this establishment]?"

105 "Now I'd like to get some information on the distribution of staff at [this establishment] across job categories. I'd like to start by reading a short list of job categories, and then go back to each category in turn and ask you for the approximate number of staff at [this establishment] in each category."

[ ]___ Management (upper & middle, not immediate supervisors)

[ ]___ Professionals

[ ]___ Sales/marketing

[ ]___ Clerical-Financial-Records

[ ]___ Production/shop floor/warehouse

[ ]___ Maintenance/janitorial

[ ]___ Full-time programmers/systems analysts/operators
[ ]___ Craftspeople and technicians
[ ]___ Other (describe)

106 How many levels of management would you describe [this establishment] as having, including both the boss and supervisors?

107 "What were the approximate annual revenues of this establishment this last year?" (If figures not available for establishment, but only for some larger unit, explain)

108 "Now I'd like to turn to information on your use of computing. Could you give me a listing of the computers presently in use at [this establishment]?"

List each machine now reported, both the kinds and numbers of each kind (only if not previously reported); strike out (on the above list) machines previously reported that are now no longer used. Where a group of machines is reported as networked, please indicate the fact. Ask: "Are any of these machines networked?"

109 "Thinking back over the years since our previous interview, how has the general business experience of your firm affected your use of computing?" (summarize discursive response)

110 "Now I'd like to learn a little about where you obtain information about possible uses of computing. In making decisions about what forms of computing to use or not to use, has [this establishment] ever relied on sources from outside the organization—for example, magazines, trade publications, vendors, competitors, or consultants?"
(If yes, record. Probe for more than one possibility.)

111 "Next I'd like your help with a checklist of activities that may or may not be computerized with you; we asked about the same list in our previous interview. For each of the following, could you indicate whether the activity is computerized or not? In some of these cases, the activity may be computerized but done for you by an outside organization, and I'd appreciate knowing about that, as well."

Note each of following with a mark for yes, no or "b" (for an outside bureau):

Financial:
[ ]___ Accounts payable
[ ]___ Invoices and billing
[ ]___ Accounts receivable
[ ]___ General ledger

[ ]___ Financial statements (balance sheet, p and l, cash flow)
[ ]___ Financial forecasting or modeling (e.g., spreadsheet)
[ ]___ Taxes and tax returns
[ ]___ Investments (tracked by computer)
[ ]___ Fixed Assets
[ ]___ Depreciation
[ ]___ Cost accounting or cost control
[ ]___ Payroll

Orders, Sales and Purchasing:
[ ]___ Order Entry
[ ]___ Job costing, pricing or estimating
[ ]___ Customer service
[ ]___ Checking of customers' credit
[ ]___ Purchase order processing
[ ]___ Sales or marketing analysis
[ ]___ Commissions on sales
[ ]___ Shipping and receiving
[ ]___ Inventory control
[ ]___ Point of sale

Manufacturing:
[ ]___ Computer-aided design (CAD)
[ ]___ Bill of materials
[ ]___ Job scheduling of tracking
[ ]___ MRP
[ ]___ Measurement of machine downtime
[ ]___ Numerically controlled machine tools
[ ]___ Computerized testing equipment
[ ]___ Scrap measurement
Paperwork:
[ ]___ Word processing
[ ]___ Mailing lists and labels
[ ]___ Records and filing
[ ]___ Graphics, charts, etc.
[ ]___ Typesetting
[ ]___ Scheduling appointments

[ ]___ Personnel records and reports

[ ]___ Tracking paperwork

[ ]___ Work measurement systems (for any category of worker)

Other

[ ]___ Networking or communication with other computers

[ ]___ Education or training

[ ]___ Scientific, engineering or R&D]

[ ]___ Other uses

PART IIA—FOR EACH APPLICATION REPORTED IN THE PREVIOUS INTERVIEW

Application #

"The next portions of the interview are organized in terms of distinct computer applications. For purposes of this study, we've defined an application as a set of activities that run off a distinct database and rely on their own software. I'd like to start by inquiring about an application that was reported in the previous interview..."

201 "Do you still have an application that does []?"

202 "What hardware does this application now run on?"

203 "What software does this application now run on?"
(Name software, if possible; make sure to note whether custom or off-the-shelf)

204 "How many staff work directly with this application, and what positions do these people hold (please classify them in terms of the categories in item 105)"
(If question arises about what we mean by "work with," let's define it as applying to those who either enter data into, or take data directly from, any computer or terminal.)

205 "Does this application do anything different now from what it was doing at the time of our previous interview?"
(If yes, record discursive response)

206 "Has there been a change in the volume of activity carried out with this application since our earlier interview?"
If yes, specify:

207 "Has the use of this application caused any changes in levels of staffing since [month, year]?"

If yes, specify (grown, shrunk, etc.).

208 "Has anyone on the staff left or been reassigned, because of this application since our last interview?" (Note: This is not identical to the previous question, which asks about total numbers of staff, rather than the allocation of specific persons to specific jobs)

(If yes, specify how many and what positions)

209 "Does this application in its present form involve any monitoring of staff performance?"

If yes, specify how. Ask "Has this changed since previous interview?"

"Next, a couple of question about relations with people and organizations outside your firm:"

210 "Have relationships with organizations or individuals on the outside in any way affected your use of this application? For example, have requirements or suggestions from suppliers, customers, creditors or others had anything to do with the way you use the application...?"

(If yes, record discursive response)

211 "Has the use of this application caused any changes in your relations with such outsiders (suppliers, customers, creditors, vendors, etc.)"

If probe seems warranted: "For example, has it put you on line with anyone outside your organization?"

PART IIB: FOR ANY APPLICATION
REPORTED DISCONTINUED:

301. "When was [   ] discontinued?"

302. "Why was it dropped?"

(Summarize discursive response; pay special attention to whether the establishment was dissatisfied with the application's performance, or whether it simply stopped doing the kind of activity for which application was employed)

303 "How many staff worked directly with this application, and what positions did these people hold (please classify them in terms of the categories in item 105)"

(If question arises about what we mean by "work with," let's define it as applying to those who either enter data into, or take data directly from, any computer or terminal.)

304 "In making the decision to drop this application, did the decision-maker(s) rely on any information from outside sources such as those I mentioned above—suppliers, customers, vendors, creditors or the like?"

If yes, summarize discursive response.

305 "Has the dropping of this application caused any changes in relations with such outsiders (customer, suppliers, vendors, or creditors, for example)?

If yes, summarize discursive response.

306 "Has the dropping of this application brought about any change in staffing levels?"

If yes, specify: Grown? Declined? By how many?

PART IIC: FOR APPLICATIONS ADOPTED
SINCE PREVIOUS INTERVIEW:

401. "What does this application do?"

402 "How long has it been up?"

403 "What hardware does it run on?

404 "What software does it run on?"

(Name software, if possible; make sure to note whether custom or off-the-shelf)

405 "How many staff work directly with this application, and what positions did these people hold (please classify them in terms of the categories in item 105)"

(If question arises about what we mean by "work with," let's define it as applying to those who either enter data into, or take data directly from, any computer or terminal.)

406 "Has the existence of this application affected staffing levels?"

(If yes, specify: Grown? Declined? By how much?)

407 "Has anyone left or been reassigned because of this application?"
(Specify what categories of staff and how many)

408 "Does this application involve any monitoring of staff performance?"
(If yes, specify)

409 "Have relationships with organizations or individuals on the outside in any way affected the creation or use of this application? For example, have requirements or suggestions from suppliers, customers, creditors, vendors or others had any effect on its development?"
(Record discursive response)

410. "Has the use of this application caused any changes in relations with such outsiders (suppliers, customers, vendors or creditors, for example)?
(If probe seems warranted: "Does it put you on-line with any outside organization?")

Bibliography

Attewell, Paul and James Rule. 1984. "Computing and Organizations: What We Know and What We Don't Know." *Communications of the ACM* 27 (12). December.

Attewell, Paul. 1994. "Information technology and the productivity paradox." In Douglas H. Harris, ed., *Organizational Linkages: Understanding the Productivity Paradox.* Washington, D.C.: National Academy Press.

Baily, Martin N. and Robert J. Gordon. 1988. "The Productivity Slowdown, Measurement Issues and the Explosions of Computer Power." *Brookings Papers on Economic Activity* 19(2): 347-420.

Bell, Daniel. 1973. *The Coming of Post-Industrial Society.* New York: Basic Books.

Braverman, Harry. 1974. *Labor and Monopoly Capital: the Degradation of Work in the Twentieth Century.* New York: Monthly Review Press.

Brynjolfsson, Erik and Lorin Hitt. 1993. "Is Information Systems Spending Productive? New Evidence and New Results." *Proceedings of the International Conference on Information Systems* 14: 47-64.

Brynjolfsson, Erik and Lorin Hitt. 1998. "Beyond the Productivity Paradox." *Communications of the ACM* 41 (8).

Brynjolfsson, Erik and Shinkyu Yang. 1998. "The Intangible Costs and Benefits of Computer Investments: Evidence from the Financial Markets." MIT Sloan School of Management.

Clemons, Eric and Michael Row. 1988. "McKesson Drug Company: A Case Study of Economost—A Strategic Information System." *Journal of Management Information Systems.* Vol. 5, No. 1.

David, Paul. 1990. "The Dynamo and the Computer: An historical perspective on the modern productivity paradox." *American Economic Review* 80(2): 355-361.

Dewan, Sanjeev and Kenneth Kraemer. 1998. "International Dimensions of the Productivity Paradox." *Communications of the ACM* 41 (8).

Dewan, Sanjeev and Chung-ki Min. 1997. "The Substitution of Information Technology for Other Factors of Production: A Firm Level Analysis." *Management Science* Vol. 43, No. 12. December.

DiNardo, John and Jorn-Steffen Pischke. 1997. "The Returns to Computer Use Revisited: Have Pencils Changed the Wage Structure Too?" *Quarterly Journal of Economics.* February.

Driscoll, J. 1982. "Office Automation: The Dynamics of a Technological Boondoggle." In *Emerging Office Systems,* edited by Robert M. Landau, James H. Bair and Jean H. Siegman. Norwood, NJ: Ablex Publishing Co.

Drucker, Peter F. 1988. "The Coming of the New Organization." *Harvard Business Review*. January-February.

Ellul, Jacques. [1954] 1964. *The Technological Society*. New York: Vintage Books.

Evans, Christopher. 1979. *The Micro-Millennium*. New York: The Viking Press.

Flaherty, David. 1989. *Protecting Privacy in Surveillance Societies*. Chapel Hill: University of North Carolina Press.

Franke, Richard H. 1987. "Technical Revolution and Productivity Decline: Computer Introduction in the Financial Industry. *Technological Forecasting and Social Change* 31: 143-1S4.

Garson, Barbara. 1988. *The Electronic Sweatshop*. New York: Simon and Schuster.

Gimlin, Debra, James Rule and Sylvia Sievers. 2000. "The Uneconomic Growth of Computing." *Sociological Forum*. Vol. 15, No. 3.

Hedstrom, Peter and Richard Swedberg. 1998. "Social Mechanisms: An Introductory Essay" in Peter Hedstrom and Richard Swedberg, eds., *Social Mechanisms*. Cambridge: Cambridge University Press.

Kling, Rob and Susan Iacono. 1988. "The Mobilization of Support for Computerization: The Role of Computerization Movements." *Social Problems* 35: 226-43.

Kling, Rob. 1996. *Computerization and Controversy; Value Conflicts and Social Choices*. New York: Academic Press.

Kraut, Robert, Susan Dumais and Susan Koch. 1989. "Computerization, Productivity, and Quality of Work-Life." *Communications of the ACM*. Vol. 32, No. 2, February.

Landauer, Thomas. 1995. *The Trouble with Computers: Usefulness, Usability and Productivity*. Cambridge, MA: MIT Press.

Laudon, Kenneth and Kenneth Marr. 1995. "Information Technology and Occupational Structure." New York University Stern School of Business Working Paper Series: IS 95 4.

Leontief, Wassily W. and Faye Duchin. 1986. *The Impacts of Automation on Employment*. New York: Oxford University Press.

Lichtenberg, Frank. 1993. "The Output Contributions of Computer Equipment and Personnel: A Firm-Level Analysis." NBER Working Paper Series No. 4540, November. Cambridge, Mass.

Morrison, Catherine and Ernst Berndt. 1991. "Assessing the Productivity of Information Technology Equipment in the U.S. Manufacturing Industries." NEER Working Paper Series No. 3582, January. Cambridge, MA.

Nolan, James. 1973 "Managing the Computer Resource: A Stage Hypothesis." *Communications of the ACM*. Vol. 16, No. 7. July.

Parsons, Julia. 1996. "Information: The Fourth Resource", in David P. Best, ed., *The Fourth Resource: Information and Its Management*. Brookfield, VT: Aslib Gower.

Pentland, Brian. 1989. "Use and Productivity in Personal Computing." *Proceedings of the Tenth International Conference on Information Systems*. ICIS, Boston, Dec. 4-6, pp. 211-222.

Powell, Walter and Paul Dimaggio, eds. 1991. *The New Institutionalism in Organizational Action*. Chicago: University of Chicago Press.

Rule, James and Paul Attewell. 1989. "What do Computers do?" *Social Problems* 36 (3).

Rule, James. 1991. "The Company Kept by Machines; Computerized Linkages among Organizations." Paper presented at SSRC Workshop on Social Science Research on Computing, Tortola, VI, June.

Rule, James and Peter Brantley. 1992. "Computerized Surveillance in the Workplace: Forms and Distributions." *Sociological Forum* 7 (3).

Scott Morton, Michael S. 1991. *The Corporation of the 1990's; Information Technology and Organizational Transformation.* New York: Oxford University Press.

Shrage, M. 1997. "The Real Problem with Computers." *Harvard Business Review* 75 (5).

Sichel, Daniel. 1997. *The Computer Revolution; An Economic Perspective.* Washington, D.C.: The Brookings Institution.

Solow, Robert. 1987. Review of *Manufacturing Matters: The Myth of the Post-Industrial Economy,* by Stephen S. Cohen and John Zysman. P. 36 in *The New York Times Book Review* (July 12).

Strassman, Paul. 1985. *Information Payoff: The Transformation of Work in the Electronic Age.* New York: The Free Press.

Tocqueville, Alexis de. [1840] 1954. *Democracy in America,* Vol. II. New York: Vintage Books.

Weiland, Ross. 1995. "2001: A Meetings Odyssey," in Rob Kling, ed., *Computerization and Controversy: Value Conflicts and Social Choices.* New York: Academic Press.

Weiland, Ross. 1996. "2001: A Meetings Odyssey," in Rob Kling, ed., *Computerization and Controversy.* New York: Academic Press.

Wiseman, Charles. 1988. *Strategic Information Systems.* Homewood, IL: Irwin Press.

Zuboff, Shoshana. 1988. *In the Age of a Smart Machine: The Future of Work and Power.* New York: Basic Books.

Index

Accounts payable and receivable, computing applications for, *see* Financial applications

Applications, *see* Computing applications

Attewell, P., 15, 22, 24, 71, 89

Authority, *see* Hierarchy, computing effects on

Autonomy, computing effects on, 53-68, 123

Bailly, M., 85-86

Bankruptcy, computing effects on, 75

Bell, D., 5-6, 70, 76, 126; *see also* Science and technology, scholarly vision of

Berndt, E., 72

Billing, computing applications for, *see* Financial applications

Bookkeeping, computing applications for, *see* Financial applications

Brantley, P., 24

Braverman, H., 5-6, 65-66, 70, 96, 116; *see also* Science and technology, scholarly vision of

Brynjolfsson, E., 71-72, 86-87

Centrone, M., 69

Clerical work, computer mediation of, 12, 65, 98-102, 113, 121-122

Cohen, S., 22

Computerization movements, 76-77

Computing: and quality improvements, 85-87; and rationalization of work, 106-113, 120, 124-127; and social change, 5-13, 115; and staff surveillance, *see* Monitoring and control of work; as image enhancement, 72, 87-88; as self-justifying enterprise, 6-7, 76-78, 123-124; change in, 33-34,

see also Computing applications, addition of, Computing applications, reduction in; decisions to adopt, 29-33, 45, 78-85, 87, 104, 115, 120, 124, 127; investment and return, *see* Cost effectiveness of computing, Returns on computing investments; lifecycle of, 44

Computing applications: addition of, 38-39, 43, 45-56; adoption in response to economic threat, 104; and collection of real-time data, 61-62, 108-113, definition of, 16; enhancement of, 40-41; fusion of, 42; multi-purpose, 35; non-standard types, 36-38; reduction in, 38, 42, 84-85, 115; sequence of adoption, 44-45, 49, 120; standard types, 33-36, 38, 47, 120; unintended uses of, 41-42, 106-107, 112, 125

Comte, A., 4-5; *see also* Science and technology, scholarly vision of

Cost-effectiveness of computing, 12, 76-90, 101, 112, 120-121

David, P., 90

Delaney, K., 22

Deskilling, 65-66, 70, 116

Dewan, S., 71

DiMaggio, P., 77; *see also* New Institutionalism

DiNardo, J., 72

Displacement of labor, 70; *see also* Employment, computing effects on

Distribution of computing functions, 34

Division of labor, *see* Deskilling

Driscoll, J., 97

Drucker, P., 98, 116

Duchin, F., 70-72, 74

Dumais, S., 67-68

Efficiency, computing effects on, 75-90, 93, 124

Ellul, J., 6-7, 76-78, 123; *see also* Computing, as self-justifying enterprise; Science and technology, scholarly vision of

Employment, computing effects on, 72, 74, 92, 118, 121-122; *see also* Clerical work, computer mediation of; Displacement of labor; Job categories, changes in

Evans, C., 9, 12

Financial applications, 17, 33-34, 36, 45, 47, 49, 120; s*ee also* Computing applications, standard types

Firm selection, *see* Sample

Flaherty, D., 64

Garson, B., 62-64

General ledger, computing applications for, *see* Financial applications

Gimlin, D., 27

Gordon, R., 85-86

Growth of computing, *see* Computing, growth of

Hedstrom, P., 117-118

Hierarchy, computing effects on, 95-98, 120; *see also* Management and structure

Hitt, L., 71

Iacono, S., 76-77

Industrial sectors: and computing use, 35-36, 47; and growth of computing, 43, 48

Information technology, *see* Computing; Computing applications

Interview: procedures, 16-19, 22-27, 53, 97; schedules, 128-140

Inventory management, computing applications for, 17, 32-33, 35, 45-47,120; *see also* Computing applications, standard types

Invoicing, computing applications for, *see* Financial applications

Isolation, 67

Job categories, changes in, 12, 97-102; *see also* Clerical work, computer mediation of; Displacement of labor

Job loss, *see* Clerical work, computer mediation of; Displacement of labor; Employment, computing effects on; Job categories, changes in

Job tracking, computing applications for, *see* Order entry and job tracking, computing applications for

Kling, R., 8, 76-77

Knowledge, new forms generated by computing, 95, 106-113

Koch, S., 67-68

Kraemer, K., 71

Kraut, R., 67-68

Landauer, T., 43, 72

Laudon, K., 97

Leontief, W., 70-72, 74

Lichtenberg, F., 71

Los Angeles Times, 1-2

Management and structure, 95-114, 116-117, 122-123

Marr, K., 97

Marx, K., 4-6, 115-116; *see also* Science and technology, scholarly vision of

Methodology, 11-12, 73; *see also* Interview, procedures; Pilot study; Sample

Middle management, computer displacement of, 97-98

Min, C., 71

Monitoring and control of work, 41, 51-68; and deskilling, 65-66; and functions of computing applications, 57-59; and sabotage, 52, 56; changes in, 59-62, 122; comprehensiveness of, 55-57, 61-61; computerized versus direct supervision, 62-64; quality of work issues, 65-68, *see also* Autonomy, computing effects on; values at stake, 62-64

Morrison, C., 72

Mythology of computing, 3; and decisions to adopt computing, 78, 88-90, 115, 121; contemporary sources, 7-10; scholarly origins, 3-7, 115-116

Myths, 3, 89

Naisbett, J., 76

National Science Foundation, 15, 19, 24